the poetry of YOGA

A CONTEMPORARY ANTHOLOGY

VOLUME 2

Edited by HAWAH

Foreword by SHARON GANNON

The Poetry of Yoga, Volume 2
First Edition

ISBN 978-1-300-30769-3

Cover design and book layout by Sascha Rossaint (www.Rossaint.com)

Cover photography of Deb Neubauer by Bill Tipper (www.BillTipper.com)

Angela Farmer's poem "Temple," was also featured in the 2013 "Yoga for the Larger Woman Calendar" produced by Vilma Zaleskaite.

WHAT THEY SAY

"Perfect for solitary contemplation, this anthology is full of yogic wisdom." **-Yoga Journal Magazine**

"This book is a link that paints an important picture and give us that experience of looking beyond appearances and feeling that profound parallel between the yogic experience and poetry." **- Rod Stryker**

"This book is the soul ignited." **- Sianna Sherman**

"Inspiring, wide ranging, humorous, thought provoking, full of wonderful imagery offering a visceral portrayal of Yoga practice: physical, emotional and spiritual. This groundbreaking volume defies simple summary. A book to cherish and revisit again and again—at home or in class." **-Jane Sill, Editor, Yoga and Health Magazine**

"Hafiz, Mirabai, Rumi, and Gibran never fail to slow speedy minds and wake closed hearts. And now, thanks to *The Poetry of Yoga,* destined to become a favorite gift book for our community, these two ancient lineages reawaken one another. These writers' words are offered as salve for the soul. May it be of benefit!"
- Waylon Lewis, Editor-in-Chief, Elephant Journal

"These beautiful poems speak to and are expressions of the very heart of yoga." - **Kelly Birch, Editor, Yoga Therapy Today**

"To have yoga without poetry is like having marriage without love. Poetry is the essence of beauty in language. I am grateful for HawaH having put together this volume to inspire yoga students with the beauty of meter and verse." **~ Aadil Palkhivala, Master Yoga Teacher**

"This collection of poems is a beautiful expression of the collective consciousness of the modern day yoga culture."
~ YOGANONYMOUS

The Poetry of Yoga

"As I started to scan through the pages, I felt like I had won the lottery! Like a beautiful asana, each page contains words perfectly aligned to lift my soul. I had been given the gift of a book of yoga poems that I know will provide inspiration for my life and my yoga classes for many years to come." **- The Daily Downward Dog**

"An exceptional compilation of poems eloquently compiled and edited by HawaH... provokes us to explore who we are, what is important in life, how we act and react to people and situations, and what it is all here to teach us." **- Maureen Miller**

"The quality and style of the poetry ranges broadly. On any given day, there will likely be something here with which anyone will resonate. And the resonances will change with each reader's own vicissitudes, making the book itself a poignantly supportive resource for practice, not to mention inspiration for one's own poetic expression. This book is a sweet gift offering to any poetically inclined yoga practitioner and a perfect item to have at yoga studios. Often, instructors will be able to bring resting students back from Savasana with an inspiring reading. *The Poetry of Yoga* offers a trove of fresh selections. Like asana practice itself, each visit to the book will bring new discovery and communion." **- Mount Shasta Magazine**

"It is such an incredible combination of yoga and poetry that we were literally 'blown away.' It has so many great poems and the offerings from the yoga community makes us proud and happy to be a part of something so special." **- Flow Yoga Magazine**

"This book is successfully building momentum to revitalize the ancient tradition of yoga poetry." **- Art of Zen Yoga**

"As if yoga and poetry were not enough to make me dance this book has it all!" **- Bikram Yoga Decatur**

"*The Poetry of Yoga* is an amazing book featuring some of today's greatest yoga teachers!" **- Opposing Views**

The Poetry of Yoga

"*The Poetry of Yoga* anthology harnesses the energy of a great movement of healing arts practitioners (as not all authors in this book are yoga teachers or practitioners and not all yoga practitioners are poets). This anthology has crossed the lines and taken the time to gather and contribute 21st century reflections of the state of an ancient practice in the modern day." **- Tribe**

"Wow, what a blessing!" **- Deheji Maat**

"If you are looking for ways to experience the art of yoga beyond the mat, be sure to read this book! And if you love poetry you won't be disappointed." **- Bay Shakti**

"I used to dream about living in the desert, where the mountains turned pink at sunset, snow graced mountain tops, and every star and galaxy in the sky opened it's glimmering eyes, now it is all here in an anthology!" **- Sister Hawk**

"Assembled by a really giving and poetic soul in HawaH. The range of voices and talents he assembled is wide and impressive. Anybody who enjoys Yoga or Poetry will enjoy this book immensely."
- Dylan Barmmer

"Granted, I don't write everyday, but I write several times throughout the week, and when I don't take that time, even five minutes, I feel off. It's the same thing when I can't get outside or don't do yoga. I get edgy, disjointed, and feel incomplete. Writing is one of the ways that I process, share, and let the Divine move through me. I suggest this trial marriage (of yoga and poetry), you'll be amazed at who and what you end up with." **- Cecilia Leigh**

"A powerhouse book of poems!" **- Where is My Guru**

"Heartwarming, funny, inspiring and enlightening. A great collection for poetry lovers—whether you practice yoga or not!"
- Chelsea Edgett

The Poetry of Yoga

"I am grateful beyond measure to be included in *The Poetry of Yoga* Anthology. The magic, grace and eloquence that fill the pages of this book are for anyone who believes in the abiding light, love and contentment we all are so blessed to embody in each breath. As a yoga teacher, no savasana will ever be the same again!"
- Jessica Durivage

"Lots of people write and read poetry and we should all come out of the closet about it." **- Mind Body Green**

"A monumental work of art, compiled and offered as a global reflection. The many poems, colors, perceptions and cadences, in *The Poetry of Yoga* together stand as one glowing source of light, one representing our generation." **- Hosh Yoga**

"Just reading many of the poems gave me a much greater desire to connect with what the practice of yoga offers!" **- Utamu Onaje**

"When you're a child and read Dr. Seuss, poetry becomes part of the childhood landscape. This is a playful, contemplative, whimsical, serious gateway back to that place. Rhyme or not, long or short, this collection of poems skewers the heart and spirit with a joyful edge. It's a must-have for any library!" **- Sherry Hanck**

"I'm impressed, there is actually a whole, budding theory on how yoga and creativity can work together in all kinds of mediums, from writing, to painting, to music, or just dealing with issues coming up in whatever work it is you do. We need creativity in all aspects of our lives, and in order to access it, we have to be willing to step out of our comfortable boxes."
- Spirituality and Health

"This book is a great victory. A voice to contemporary yoga. Through this book we get to see the somatic power of consciousness."
- Shiva Rea

"Life is too short to make just one decision

Music's too large for just one station

Love is too big for just one nation and

God is too big for just one religion."

-MICHAEL FRANTI

CONTENTS

The Poetry of Yoga

The **Poetry** of **yoga**

TIME

The Poetry of yoga

The Poetry
of Yoga

The Poetry of yoga

RELATIONSHIP

DESTINY

The Poetry of Yoga

The Poetry of Yoga

The Poetry of Yoga

PROLOGUE

Volume 2! This wasn't even supposed to happen. When I started accepting online submissions of poetry for the book, in October 2010, I wasn't even sure if I would get enough good material for one book. Contrary to my expectations, over the next six months I received over 1,500 pages of poetry from 19 countries. There came a point, during the final week of submissions, when over 35 poems were submitted each day! I officially closed submissions on April 15, 2011. And then reopened submissions for 3 months in the beginning of 2012; another 500 pages of poetry poured in from around the world.

From the beginning, I wanted to help kick-start and harness a modern day renaissance of Hafiz, Mirabai, and Rumi. I figured I could do this through expanding the literary tradition of yoga to include the cultural perspective of the 21st century. Most of the celebrated mystic poet yogis have long been deceased. I envisioned the book as a platform for a new body of work reflecting on how yoga continues to shift the landscape of human consciousness and civilization. A book anthology of modern-living poetic voices who simply needed a platform to share their existential expressions.

To supplement and excite people about the idea, I asked living master teachers and writers from around the world to also contribute poetry to the project. I wanted to get their voices in the mix, and sent invitation letters over email to those I knew. I planned to integrate and combine the words of established teachers with everyday people, as well as participants who attended *The Poetry of Yoga* workshops that I was teaching.

Another one of my goals was to encourage yoga teachers and students to step out of their comfort zones and write poetry, even

if they had never done so in the past. I began fishing for poetry from the far reaches of the globe—posting the International Call for Submissions on websites, listserves, and using social marketing tools to get the word out. Almost immediately a litany of emails started coming in through the comments page on the website; personal emails I received from people expressed the project inspired them to write their first poem ever; others spoke to the timeliness of such an anthology. What began as a one-human guerrilla operation became a poetic movement, harnessing social media as a tool to unite us across physical boundaries.

The reading of all the poetry that came in was an absolute pleasure and joy. It was an honor to have my finger on the pulse of such creative, soul inspiring, and mystical poetry from around the world. It took months—and now, almost two years, to read the work over and over again.

After reading and sorting the work into large piles through an internal system of poetic theme and quality, I began to move poetry from pile to pile and slowly narrowed the work down to 600 pages; still too much for one book! It seemed unfair to try and limit the work to one anthology. So I decided to turn the submitted poetry into two anthologies and make use of this opportunity to broadcast to the world all these tremendous poetic voices. Inside the two book set are poems from Argentina, Sri Lanka, Ireland, Philippines, China, Wales, Guatemala, India, Norway, U.S.A., Australia, Japan, Pakistan, Romania, Mexico, England, Venezuela, South Africa, Brazil, and Canada.

Now, the final part of the mission is for this anthology to raise money for the dynamic work of a great non-profit organization called One Common Unity. Ultimately, I hope the project will provide a sustainable source of revenue for the work they

The Poetry of Yoga

HawaH

have been doing since the year 2000. One Common Unity supports a movement for peace education and the building of a non-violent culture through music and art. Specifically, they facilitate arts-based health and wellness, conflict resolution, and nonviolence education for inner-city youth.

Spiritual warriors, compassionate renegades, lovers of truth and seekers of wisdom... the time is now. Let these words breathe through the pores of your skin. Let your mind stir, the hairs on your arms stand, and let this be a reminder that we have not lost our souls.

Read in awe and wonder, as I did... I hope you do, embrace all the magical poetry in this collection. Take it around the world with you and let it serve proof of the modern day poetic soul of humanity.

Your Reflection,

HAwAH

The Poetry of Yoga

Sharon Gannon

FOREWORD

You hold in your hands, the second volume of *The Poetry Of Yoga*, a collection of poems written by contemporary yogis, and compiled by visionary yogi poet HawaH, who, in elegant and succinct simplicity worthy of the ancient rishis, proclaims the poet's desperate yearning to evolve in a poem entitled *Destiny:*

We are the water
Before it gains a reflection
The snail
That wished to move faster
A fish
That desired to walk on land
A stone that desired to feel

HawaH feels the urgency and the need to facilitate the expression of poetry into the world today. He knows without a doubt something of the power of the spoken word to elicit positive change, to break the chains that hold our hearts and minds in isolated prisons of disconnection. He feels the healing approaching and has accepted the role of leader—a fearless leader who believes that to read is to empower and to empower is to write and to write is to influence and to influence is to change. And change we must: morphing into our future selves, wild and free, able to perceive beauty in all things and most importantly able to express and embody that beauty as ourselves.

In a world that elevates technology and left-brain thinking over the arts—yoga and poetry enter the global field boldly. One might ask, *Is there a place for poetry and yoga in our world today? Why should we pay attention to what the yogi poets have to say?* These are valid questions that can best be answered by immersing oneself in the reading and writing of

The Poetry of Yoga

Sharon Gannon

poetry and in the practice of yoga. Both poetry and yoga are, after all, experiential disciplines—theorizing and philosophizing about them, or even merely trying to explain what they are, have a place, but such intellectual pursuits can never lead to full understanding. Poetry and yoga are practices of reductionism, in which the practitioner attempts to strip away that which is superfluous to arrive at the essential.

In this recognition lies a possible answer to the relevance of poetry and yoga to the world today. Our present world culture promotes consumerism—encouraging the acquiring of more and more stuff—while, yoga and poetry are about letting go at all levels. Yogis and poets strive to feel comfortable with the apocalyptic experience—the experience of standing naked, in the words of Bob Dylan, "like a creature devoid of form," the form being the cloak of culture that obscures and disconnects us from the essential truth about ourselves and others. Yogis and poets are most comfortable in a place where essential feeling takes precedence over intellectual, literal meaning. The 14th-century Persian mystic poet Hafiz makes this point metaphorically:

> A poet is someone
> Who can pour Light into a spoon,
> Then raise it
> To nourish
> Your beautiful parched, holy mouth.
> *(translation Daniel Landinsky)*

Yoga and poetry have a luminous shared history. *Who knows this?* is a line in the *Rig Veda*, an ancient Sanskrit scripture, written in poetic form, dealing with the big questions: *Who am I?, Who are you?, What is this?, Where did we come from?,* and *Where are we going?* The line *Who knows this?* appears as both a question and an answer, defying direct meaning, presenting itself as a riddle. By solving the riddle you discover

The Poetry of Yoga

Sharon Gannon

who you are—the ultimate goal of spiritual practice. Both poetry and yoga move from the outer to the inner—acknowledging the here and now and from that place moving inside to subtler realms of causal being. As George Harrison sang, "It's so far-out, the way out is in." Like the *Rig Veda*, all mystical poetry has the potential to liberate you from who you think you are, or what you think something is, and magically shift your perception to reveal who you and everything else might be.

Where does poetry begin? If you have never written a poem before, where do you start? You start with a feeling, a deep, persistent and desperate feeling to know. Then immerse yourself in poetry. Read poems written by other people. Read the poems in this book. Start with page one and read through to the end. Stop now and then and try writing a poem of your own in a blank space. If the inspiration to write is hard coming, then keep reading until you get desperate enough.

When I read poems I get the encouragement to write poems. When I read poems my brain opens to let in the words, which mingle intimately with the mess of my mind and the ache of my heart, giving me something to stand upon—a solid place to step off from into possibility—if I want to. Fleeting fragments and unfinished sentences can speak more truth than volumes of clearly constructed essays or instruction manuals. I love the feeling of being washed over and through with poems—unspeakable teasing and tempting, the unquenchable yearning of my body, my soul, my self.

There is nothing more inspiring for poet than to listen to poetry. Yes, I mean poems written by other people. Other people's poems can push a poet deeper into the inarticulate, murky, hard-to-reach places, allowing the poet to catch a glimpse, which they will naturally and unapologetically devour, digest

and transform alchemically into words of their own. I think this is wonderfully expressed in a poem in this anthology entitled *Words*, by Lois Read:

> Words resound in my soul like gongs
> or the bells in the Buddhist temple...
> Words bounce like lottery balls in a wire cage
> wake me from a sound sleep
> crying out "use me, use me!
> *(excerpt taken from page 48)*

We live in a human society that is very head oriented, as if the body were just something used to transport the head from place to place. In contrast, the yogi poets write from a whole body experience, celebrating the joining of the physical with the cerebral and mystical, rejoicing in their inseparability.

I am in awe of the poems in this book. I am in awe of the gatherer of these poems. I am in awe of yoga, the mystery that can never be completely fathomed, the bottomless pit that is emptiness. I am enjoying being in awe. Don't get me wrong—my awe is no sedentary, mute bewilderment. My awe is quite desperate. Poems are desperate, and who can pass up desperation? It is very attractive and begs to be paid attention to. Please pay attention to these desperate poems. Read them and then allow them to push you past the time it took to get to the place where you are now. Then write some of your own before you find that you are tired, and in the words of HawaH, *weighted down and exhausted from holding so many moments.*

- Sharon Gannon

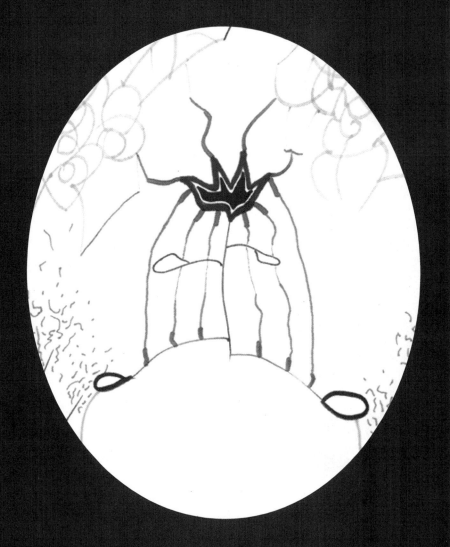

LIGHT

The clouds converse
Over a glass of sunset
The sky is drunk
From light

The Poetry of Yoga

Lulu Ekiert

OPENING

Suffering is
the distance between
me and myself,
and only practice brings me back.
These days
I practice
sitting,
straight and even,
breathing,
slow and deep,
waiting,
patiently,
until I'm ready
to let go
of last time,
of next time,
and become
with every cell of my being
this time.

The Poetry of Yoga

Megan Merchant

DEAR UNIVERSE,

Keep a prayer for peace
in your night stand
addressed to the Universe.

Open it when the death toll
reaches a number higher
than you can imagine
in jelly beans.

Drive to the outskirts of town,
turn left at the motel where
you would never spend the night.

The one seeded with shower
curtain mold, fiber sheets, cable TV.

Roll down your window,
feel the nuzzle of desert air
soften your collarbones.

Look closely for a field of sunflowers
and release your well worded plea.
Feel effective, compassionate.
A ripple, maybe, in the cosmos.

Drive home believing
an African woman
was spared rape,
her children untied from a tree.

The man on the ledge stepped back,
returned home to kiss his wife.

A vice president requested a moment
of silence in the middle of a meeting
so that an entire office
could connect to their breath.

If you believe this is possible,
keep reading. Spend the next ten seconds
in the white space of your own prayer.

SO HUM

I need a wood floor
and a mat.
I need a god in the room
and a teacher reminding me to breathe.
Any god. Every breath.
I need to feel my side ribs move,
my feet ground and lift, ground, lift.
I need my belly to hollow
and hips slide open.
I need my spine to extend
and fold, gracefully.
I need the breath to make room.
Exhale. Release. Pause.
I need to give everything
away that I need
and vibrations to dance on the hum of my so-hum.
I am *so hum* that I am *so hum*.
I am *so hum* that I am *so hum*.
I don't need a teacher
or language
to remind me,
there's a god in the room
giving away everything
with her breath.

BEFORE SUNRISE

Once, through moth-eaten tears
in a half-remembered dream,
you promised that the sun would
discard its tarnished shell.

You said it would slither out of
its skin and swamp us with hope.

That I'd recognise the day
by the taste of the sky;
that I'd wake up to smell sunlight
soaking me like coffee baths.

I remember the picture you painted
whilst your gnarled hands shook
with the hope of imminent hope;
the canvas reflected in your eyes,
a day when I wouldn't have to breathe to live.
When my rusty chains would chain themselves.
When I'd walk out of my skin without being naked.
When the words I'd speak would be the ones I'd formed.

You said, son, this is not hope that you carry into time;
it's hope you must possess and master.
For when the raindrops have turned to mist,
and the tear-stained grass has gone to dust,
love, as breathless as a running sun, will arrive again.

Qty.	Content ID	Description	Page Count
1	12922311	The Poetry of Yoga (Vol. 2)	334

Printed, bound, and packed with care at Lulu.com

Have a question about your order? Reach our support team at www.lulu.com/support, or call us toll-free at 1-844-212-0689

Shipment Summary

Lulu Press, Inc.
627 Davis Drive
Suite 300
Morrisville, NC 27560

Received by:
Gabrielle Weber

900 Mulberry Street

Louisville, KY 40217   United States

BLOSSOMING

In the beginning,
With each unraveling of the mat,
We are anxious to add to our garden,
To gather the beautiful buds,
And coax each asana to open quickly.
Feet in the dirt we stand,
Sometimes for the first time,
Connecting earth to muscle and muscle to sky,
The energy of an immense lineage
Pulsing with promise.
But as the poses settle,
As we settle,
We find that yoga's true gift is not about more
But less.
The outline of the poses remain the same,
Yet when the space between is fed,
When ease replaces expectation,
When patience replaces petals,
We find that the asanas are no longer
About holding on,
But about letting go.
And in that release,
Without judgment or force to impede,
Breath floods in,
Releasing the mind and freeing the heart.
Through yoga,
We find
That core of serene nothingness,
And learn that in letting go,
We gain everything.

The Poetry
of Yoga

Naveen Thomas

ILLEGIBLE

This soft, spider-webby feeling
on my forehead
tells me I'm onto something good.
So what if it is illegible.

STRICTLY
CONFIDENTIAL

The story of my hips is strictly confidential.
Locked up tighter than tight.
I'd like to place an order for a me-shaped key.

OPENING TO GRACE

In my practice
in my life
I have planted seeds of hope
been rooted in faith
witnessed the tender new growth
of my awareness
and tended to my practice
like a master gardener
honoring every tight little bud
beginning to emerge
Only when I began to serve
did my yoga blossom
Petal by petal unfolding
Opening to grace

I no longer seek the perfect pose
An end result
the skilled gardener, a prized bloom
I honor the flaws, frayed edges,
dark spots, shadow side
fragmented reflection of light
And another petal unfurls
Opening to grace

I till the soil and gather the seeds
of knowledge to offer my community
A wisdom beyond my own
with my authentic voice
To be of service, to learn and teach
We weed our gardens and mindfully plant our
intentions
To witness our physical bodies and minds
Yoking with the subtle energetic body
We yearn for the light
Like wildflowers and stately trees
Shrubs, moss and climbing roses
Opening to grace

DROPBACK TO LOVE

Strength in every fiber
I root deep and bend unwound
Arms succumb to float
like freed leaves, earthbound

I am fearless and vulnerable in my offering
A prayer without a sound
May my heart crack wide
Like thawing ice
the moment I touch the ground

Grace in the arms of a beautiful friend
I may never see again
But for today, in time and space
I trust you right away

Find your love, embrace your love
Then give it all away

Terilyn Wyre

HOUSEHOLDER

Remembering our first meditations
Of tiny suckling rhythms, peach fuzz sensation
and newborn scent.

No need for my mat in those early weeks our sacred
shared space was my practice, more familiar than my own,
the rise and fall of your breath.

But years have passed by and we grow in unexpected ways.
I have worn holes in my mat yearning to experience my
authentic practice; to feel sacred space all my own;
to find meditation; but no quiet mind here for this householder.

I love you with every prana filled cell of my being, pure
and true yet the fuel of my suffering, attachment to
you challenges every notion I have of evolving.

I dream of running away. Bali.
Where dedicating my existence to God is less conditional.
Without the frayed edges of a strained marriage
and a child's diagnosis of behavioral disorder.
Maybe there they would accept you with compassion
without labels, where all children have special needs.

I doubt disorders run rampant in Bali
Maybe it's beautifying your surroundings for God
Maybe it's the sun
Maybe it's acceptance
Maybe it's Michael Franti and yoga and music
and culture that means something

Maybe it's time I go meditate and teach class
and look to the yogis and the community I am in
for the inspiration to stay present in the life I have chosen.

WORDS

Words resound in my soul like gongs
or the bells in the Buddhist temple
where the saffron clad boy monk
sidled close to me on the wooden bench
to see what I was sketching.

Words bounce like lottery balls
in a wire cage
wake me from a sound sleep
crying out,
"Use me, use me!"

Words are what the poet sings
off-key and on
to celebrate the everyday
the cosmic and the comic
the chorus of the universe.

Words. Placed by the poet in a certain way
tweak the ear and the heart
to sidle close
to listen carefully
as the world pours in.

PEPPER IN CHOCOLATE

The butterfly is busy
doing its appointed thing,
sipping nectar from the blooms
on the butterfly bush,
natural order underscored.

Yet what of the maverick—
the butterfly who dares to try
the wildness of the fireweed?
The gourmet who flirts with a flavor
as unlikely and delicious
as pepper in chocolate?
The young engineer
who turns the world upside-down
in a California garage?

Where does dreaming fit
in the blueprint for the universe?
On the edge perhaps, just off the page?
Or underlying everything,
written with invisible ink...

EXCHANGE

I listen to ocean music outside the villa's window
all night and dream it's a recording of the ocean
playing in an endless loop lulling me to sleep
I dream your body's a recording of a body
weaving endless around my body in discordant loop.

I dream the pink buoys are recordings of buoys.
When you reach to grasp them in a moment of survival,
they pop like birthday balloons mocking your need of breath.
I dream I drink the ocean and I do not drown.
I remain alive and thirsty.

In the morning you say
so we'll spend Passover alone
and your birthday alone. Yes.
We'll remain in exile, unborn, uncelebrated.

We met the ends of love on a dark island
full of palm trees, coconuts and rum.

Tomorrow the long ride on the dirt road
straight to the Montego Bay Airport,
the runway, the final ascent.

When we touch ground
it will be over. As usual,
people will applaud their own survival.

The Poetry of Yoga

Lisa Grunberger

SHE GIVES THANKS TO CHILDREN IN THE PARK

Thank apples for snakes,
thank snakes for knowledge.

Thank mirror for distortion,
thank frame for preservation.

I thought I would keep you,
but you fell apart, flew away.

I will not bind myself to joy
but to Isaac's laughter,
his swinging legs clasped
around the branch of his favorite tree.

I will not blind myself
to the flying kisses he casts,
into the dark future of a girl
standing by a tunnel,
tattooed with graffiti they can not yet read,
the tunnel where the moonlight hides
in shame for each letter's ink is still wet.

I will not wait for the angel either,
but grow my own wings,
stutter away into the appled sun.

Dr. James Gordon

TRAUMA HEALING IN HAITI

Already 9am.
The air is hot and heavy in the workshop tent.
Fifty or sixty people are present, most of them quite young,
taking notes, wonderfully attentive and responsive.

They are a bit shy at first,
but as we all introduce ourselves,
they offer stories of trembling bodies, panicked hearts,
of sights beyond endurance...
watching family members crushed under falling concrete.

I talk with them about fight-or-flight and stress;
they become animated, calling up the unspeakable terror
of the earthquake along with the biological facts
and personal experience.

Trauma can produce the symptoms of ongoing stress:
difficulty concentrating, sleeplessness, anger, lethargy,
flashbacks of death and destruction.

The techniques we use teach slow deep breathing,
self-expression and self-discovery in drawings,
healing through sharing one's pain and hopes with others.

Moving one's body can give relief;
restore a sense of calmness, provide perspective,
grant a sense of control,
open the door to the possibility of a future.

The Poetry of Yoga

Dr. James Gordon

Explaining imagery and encouraging them to draw,
the young women are alive with pleasure and discovery.

They share first with each other,
and then with the whole group.

They show us pictures bisected by the barriers
between the living and the dead,
whom they miss so much,
and then more drawings that reveal the possibility
of feeling whole again
in nature and with family and friends.

By the time we clear away the chairs and begin to shake,
the girls are waving their arms and laughing.
When Bob Marley's "Three Little Birds" comes on,
they sing with him, and us.

They are filled with sunlight after darkness;
with music, drums, guitar, dance and movement,
after "the biggest problem"
of buried and walled off emotions,
broken bodies and silence
is traversed.

Some of us are still laughing, others crying in release,
with gratitude as well as grief.

The Poetry of Yoga

Laura Zamfir

IN A LIFETIME
WE ALL CHANGE

Our age | Most of us change:
Body's appearance | Our address
Hair style | Our e-mail
Activities | Our phone
Habits | Our city
Customs | Our country
Points of view | Our continent
Values | Our nickname
The entire blood in 21 days | Our name
All cells including bones, in | Our social status
7 years | Our profession
and more... | Our culture
| And more

But with all these changes,
we can't get lost anyway
because there is one thing that never changes,
carrying through eternity, our identity.
Did you ever wonder what that is?

It is Your Light Within.

stretching yoginis and buddhas
line the stairs
incense rising
yoga studio hot as hell
i'm in heaven

HEAVEN

The Poetry of Yoga

David Newman

HEARTSONG

It's time for healing, time to have faith
Time for living with trust in God's Grace
Time for releasing all the things that you fear
Listen to your heart and tell me what you hear
Time for giving and time to believe
Time to reap harvest time to receive
There's no time for wasting with happiness so near
Listen to your heart and tell me what you hear
On a journey of a lifetime
Above the noises of the crowd
In the throws of passion's fire
Can you reach the higher ground?
Oh can you feel it, isn't it clear?
Listen to your heart. Tell me what you hear
It's time for kindness, compassion and care
Time to take action, be bold and aware
Time to move forward while your vision is clear
Listen to your heart. Tell me what you hear
Amidst the cries for freedom
On the wings of prayer
For the hunger, the desire, to feed a soul lost in despair
Oh can you feel it, isn't it clear?
Listen to your heart and tell me what you hear
My heart song sings love each other
My heart sings see God in the other
My heart song sings love each other
See God in the other
Be kind and live as one

TO BE HOME

I have been hiding out
I have been holding on
Like a bird in the ocean, looks up to the sky
Been Bound to my freedom
Been crawling on high
It's been such a long time
Since your heart has felt mine
Down the straight and the narrow
With wings I would fly
As the path fades before me
I just let it go by
To be home with you again
All alone with you again
Measuring distance beyond space and time
What I haven't lost, I will never find
I'll be on my way now
Let this old wheel keep spinning round
From a drop of your water
To a grain of your sand
From the distance between us
Back to the touch of your hand
To be home with you again
All alone with you again
All that I've chosen and all that I fear
I must carry on now
Please wait for me here
To be home with you again
All alone with you again

WITH ALL YOUR NERVES

drop into the room
in your body

explore the old pain that keeps hiding
behind stories

and like blood returning to frost bitten flesh
wake up

don't keep steering down the same
street where there are no children playing

turn, with all your nerves, to work
where your terror is tucked away

the diamond is amongst the hardest rock
and the pearl sinks to the ocean bottom

enclosed within its shell

THE WAY 'ROUND

we have birthed a thousand children
birthed each other
sucked each the others' breasts
our children's children even
loved the others' mother seen the fathers die
as you and I
an ocean cried between us
and with as many words
we have loved a million times and held each other so
and hated
and more

died in each other's arms again
as mother/father/sister/brother/lover
and wished never to have happened
that moment
when we said again
goodbye
again

and when words and sight and touch arouse
the small place in which we meet/have ever met
we come 'round again

and laugh
and cry
and birth
and die
again, again, again

THE HONEY BEES WET INK

Wish for it.
Sit still beneath the boughs
of the tree you read about, in books,
mapped out and eulogized in the east.
Let it fill with rain, then snow, water talk,
rivers flow into other rivers with names like
life-blood of god, endless curls of the beloved,
sappy spring rising through branches,
just like water makes pathways through earth,
it should make the body flower with eventual bloom.
You become the tree.
40 days of no fruit.
No color: as from the world
the most incredible saffron sunlight pours
from a sky so blue you could eat.
But do not touch this.
Do not reach out for it.
The beloved tempts you, serenades you with adagios
written for saints.
The primal word sets traps for you
as notes from a flute.
But do not listen.
Enjoyable figs, juice from the mango,
ruby pomegranate seeds sparkle before you.

You hunger for it but remain still.
Who is she who raises her arms,
thumbs folded over two fingers in mudra,
lightning language of the body sifting through mind,
repeating the mantra at the forehead
so that the heart bursts open?
So it could catch fire, and wake all those who sleep
beneath sleeping trees in a forest where
no one knows the answer to the koan
of the sound of a tree falling
where no one is listening.
Remain in posture, breathe, repeat the mantra.
Let it vibrate the point
between the eyebrows.
Earth as my witness, the world went white.
Held back a thousand arrows,
a thousand earthquakes,
a thousand tidal waves,
by the finger of the woman
sitting beneath the tree
resting on earth.
Time and time again, I try to come to you.
But the earth holds on to me here.
I remain still, floating still
in the honey bees wet ink.

The Poetry of Yoga

Lara Sookoo

AUM

watching the drop of clear dew
turn to red flame with the
new born sun
brightest moment before death
it evaporates

hands touching in
the moment of forever
more fleeting than tears
essence of it
remains for lifetimes

inspired by the mud
at its roots

watching the master
in meditation
immovable as the dark
fragile as a breeze
the peace of
inspiration

how the lotus glows
among dark water plants
against the surface of
the pond
beauty aching for light

writing a thousand
lines
only to discover a word
that is less
than the mind
more than the universe

aum

The Poetry of Yoga

Nicole Argento
Gonzalez

OCTOPUS

my heart is cracked
like an earthquake its parts crumble,
sever and scatter
you, and solely you,
catch the whirling pieces;
weld and sew and glue
fiercely mending into the red night,
the moon and stars iridescent
gleam, glow and glitter

i feel the wind on my face
i feel altered and transformed
i feel the tentacles of life
spreading and growing and pulling
it back together, so it can beat,
blood vibrant and strong
and

i

can
breathe
again

RUN AND RACE

Chase chase chase,
the elusive one thing
that's gonna make it better.

That if only "I" had this!
One thing in my life.

Is akin to a rock wishing to be the rain,
all the while,
missing and dismissing every rain drop
that stopped to visit and lovingly
caress its face.

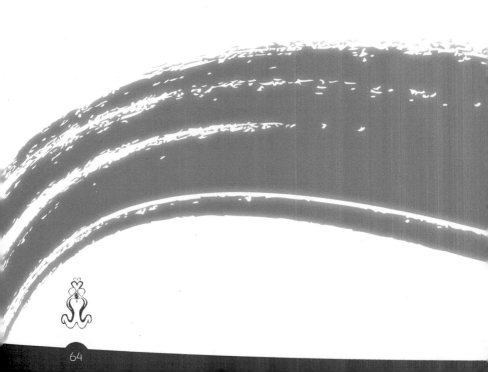

THE SPIRIT OF YOGA

When you feel the Spirit move you
Quietly from within,
You will sense a spark of silence;
A vibration will begin.

Now the veinous tide subsiding
Calms the sanguinary rush,
And the heart begins to whisper
'Til you barely hear the hush.

And the mind explodes with brilliance
In the rapture of the Light.
It is yours to keep forever
But not by holding tight.

The Poetry of Yoga

Heather Barfield

in yoga class today
the young,
hot teacher spoke
in a nonchalant way
about balance between
effort and ease

BETWEEN EFFORT AND EASE

i sob in pigeon
whimper in plank
shake in dancer
recover in child

hips on fire!
breath to heated pain
located deep
subterranean muscle bone flesh
years of denial
pent up desire
implanted Puritan programs
patriarchal possession
priests, popes, professors
and all the other 'p's
controlling, contriving and conjuring

against the Truth of Me

i follow my heart
love as i please
most especially
inwardly, intimately

The Poetry of Yoga

Heather Barfield

yearning to solve riddles
etched in sand
under Sphinx's claws

ignored, as usual...
my voice too tainted with trouble

meanwhile i carve space for others
measuring risk against risk
unraveling knots
complexes tied in bundles
which is this one?
any day now
any day now

fear destroying friendships
meant to grow
opportunities slipping past
heart of iron
heavy to hold
water boiling
about to pop...

swan dive down
plank, upward dog, downward dog
breathe
warrior one, warrior two
breathe

waiting.
balancing
effort and ease.

The Poetry of Yoga

Stacey Steinbach

breathe
stretch
move
breathe
breathe
thoughts
thoughts
I am in my head
what's going on
what do I need to do tomorrow
what's for dinner
breathe
breathe
focus
must focus
am I doing this right
my body does not move like theirs
breathe
breathe
breathe
that's not comfortable
my body does not move like that
this hurts
but I want to do it like they are doing it
adjust
adjust
relax
breathe
it will be ok
it is ok
I can move how I need to move
relax

breathe
breathe
if I do this now I will be relaxed
for tomorrow
stop thinking about relaxing
breathe in and out, out and in
it is ok
my body moves how it is
supposed to move
breathe
open heart
release the day's stress
breathe
breathe
breathe
grace
appreciate the practice where
I am at
breathe
breathe
breathe
breathe
breathe
gratitude
love
light
shine
heart
wisdom
open
open
open
breathe

THE PRACTICE

The Poetry
of Yoga

Victor van Kooten

SHORT POEM

HE was right
So
she left.

The Poetry of Yoga

Victor van Kooten

OPEN UP

Unwrap this present
from its complex-soft container,
born onto the straw that carried grain.
his body turned to bread,
his blood became the wine.
spread far and wide
over your dining table.
when it is all gone,
left in the empty space,
remains the presence of the maker.
feminie teachings
from the hole inside
your visible ear,
like unseen wind passing
in and out of your breathing chest,
the round shape
the earth you stand upon.
become the arches of your feet.
your hollow palms
around the nothingness
you will never catch...
open up.

GATEWAY OF THE HEART

The walls stained, scuffed and bruised
Playful heart centered loving and free
Our love, the kula and me
Love abounds, quieting my mind to hear a divine sound
Joy unfolding as we chant
A grace which brightens a light into this home of ours
A kula happy loving and free
Light the way
Showing us our hearts
Own destiny
Gratitude explodes from my soul
Each face, each loving heart
Reaching out to help a friend in need
As our bodies brighten, aligning
Into the currents of grace and love
We see ourselves brilliant, shining, radiant divine vessels
Peace makers within
A helpful community of love
The purpose of this practice deepens us within
The vein of love
Which we all share
Brings us together again
One love
Into the world of longing
Our hearts finally belonging
Integrating us all through the gateway of our hearts

The Poetry of Yoga

Christy Nones
Mckenzie

THE ALCHEMY
OF HATHA

Defining Hatha inspires *wonder.*

The poetic: Ha/Tha - Sun/Moon
A harmonious balance of opposites,
uniting body, mind and heart.

The literal: Ha-tha   'Forceful Strike'
From Alchemical Tantric traditions
in medieval India,
a powerful tool uniting body, mind and heart.

The wonder:
How is it, through this odd and ancient practice,
struck forcefully with blazing challenge,
I come to peaceful clarity of acute presence?

Seems the needle-point lucidity of mind
—what is priority and worthy of focus—
is whittled sharp by the blows
of pain, loss or crisis.

The wonder:
How is painful darkness the perfect womb
to incubate the light of gratitude?

Seems in the shadows there are no distractions;
No exit from feeling.
Swaddled in difficulty,
the mind's attention becomes bright.

The Poetry of Yoga

Christy Nones
McKenzie

The wonder:
How is clear, sharp knowing
expertly forged and fashioned
through smoldering intensity of sensation?

Seems being engulfed in the flames of every nuance
on the burning edge of my body's potential,
I quiver and boil in a cauldron of discomfort.

Struck by the loss of my ego's sovereignty,
feeling agony and pain of melancholy muscles,
absorbed in crisis of self-doubt and limitation,
what is most sublime rises to the top of my brew.

The wonder:
Is it the impact of ceasing distractions that shifts aimless
awareness into sharpened meaning?

Seems with a flash of cool breath,
comes precise, deep knowing.
Threads of my Heart's peaceful wisdom
pierce the agitated eye of mind
in a pointed, inexplicable moment...

Alchemy.

The Poetry
of Yoga

Carol Murphy

BADDHA KONASANA

Spine folds and forehead rests on toes,
Feet, that hold the imprint of my history,
That have walked my life's trajectory,
And will lead me to my destiny,
Humbly curl onto my brow,
Witnessing the now.

The same feet that have walked from confrontation,
Stumbled from misfortune,
And stood back up again.
Instinctively knowing when.

The same feet that connect me to this earth,
Where my ancestors once stood, in the eternity of now.
The shadow of their footprints furrows in my brow.
To their silhouette I bow.

MAYA

Living in the illusionary world of dualism and separation,
Where the wisdom of the dharmic laws have suffered denigration,
And governments and corporations dictate psychotic legislation,
Based on the fundamental failings of greed and exploitation.

Living in the illusionary world of dualism where the truth of the dharma is lost,
And we live separated from the natural order unaware of the karmic cost,
Our Consciousness divided and torn miroring our spiritual regression.
The sacred earth raped daily as an act of global aggression,
Dysfunctional environmental ethos renamed as progression.

Living in the illusionary world of dualism
Where mind and body are not seen as a single entity,
But separate and severed in a schizophrenic identity,
Where God or the absolute is seen as something disconnected,
Not the sacred reality of the natural world needing to be protected.

Living in the illusionary world of dualism there is no hope or resolution,
No unity or equanimity,
No spiritual evolution.
It is all one, the rest is delusion,
It is all one, the rest is confusion.

The truth is simple: Step outside of this imaginary world and be a part of the solution.

NEEM KAROLI BABA

This poem is not fancy, I know
but listen carefully:
something is there.

My friends have their houses
and I guess that's okay.
But this is an eternal house.
Never needs painting.
Roof never leaks.

Why did Neem Karoli Baba
lie there naked on a blanket
smiling like a walrus
while Ram Dass took his photo?

What were his clothes and belongings?
What was his roof and awning?
What was his porch and railing?
If it wasn't This,
what was it?

That's what this poem is like
unadorned figures of speech,
not costumed by poetic diction

plain speech and metaphor
wrapped only in a light skin,
no ego world to cloud
the natural shining effulgence.

I myself am flopped out in this poem,
bare-bottom,
with a long-toothed grin,
nothing of myself but listener and scribe
no erudition or wit
Mind at the service
of the great Creator.

As Sixth Zen Patriarch Hui-Neng said:
The bottom of a pail
is broken through.
Personal contents have gone out.

FASTING

If you don't eat,
the day stretches out empty in front of you,
not a damn thing to do.

You better eat your peas!
I don't think so. Not today.
I'm busy with something else.

Sorry, Mommy.
Not that you haven't given me everything.
But this is a day for deductions.
Subtraction. Mathematics.
Everything take away everything leaves what?
That's right everything.
Hmmm. I'm beginning to figure it out.

I want to be thin and emaciated,
a starving lover walking the streets of Paris
wearing a top hat and tattered tails and
carrying a beat-up cane,
pacing late at night below the balcony
of his beloved,
expecting only a glimpse of light,
the smallest ray,
as she glances through the louvered door.

But there is nothing!
And in torture and disappointment and agony
he lays down in the street
waiting for the wheels of a carriage
to end it all.

Then suddenly the downstairs door is thrown open,
light everywhere,
suffering disappears as if it had never existed,
he rushes in,
knocking off his hat into the street.

He throws the cane and cape
out into the street with it,
he doesn't need them anymore.

Later a poor, destitute
hunchback comes down the street,
thrilled, he picks up the stuff, puts it on,
walks to his girl's apartment,
the same damn thing happens.
And so on.

The cape and cane are yours now, aren't they?
Be like the lover. Be like the hunchback.
The body doesn't matter.
When the lights go on, you're in another room.
A much roomier one.

Or be like me, a hungry,
ratty little bookkeeper,
who eventually takes away everything
and stands in his own being.
At first you think you've made
a grievous mistake
in calculation, your eyes water over,
you worry your master will beat you,
you will lose your post,
your wife, your beloved children,
scrubby as they are,
but your vision shifts,
from the object to the background,
from the thing to the nothing,
and you become an artist,
an artist of emptiness.

Sacre Bleu. Enchante'.
Say hello to yourself.
A quelle heure est le diner?
Let's get some real food.

The Poetry of Yoga

MC Yogi

SHIVA (SUPREME SOUL)

Supreme Fountain head with the mounted dread
with the one ton drum lord of the grateful dead
wed to the earth always covered in ash
may your power reign down from Mount Kailash

Full moon eclipse swallow the darkness
taste bliss let it drip from your third eye lid.
Slip into a trance see the whole world dance
shine down from the crown like an avalanche

GANESHA (SOUND THE HORN)

Break through the surface burn through the shell
the mind is a maze gotta shine through the veil
trapped in jail and you swallowed the key
you're the only one who can set yourself free

clear the debri, sweep rocks from the road
let go feel the soul start to overflow
tidal wave full of grace wash through the mind
crush every thought back into light

burn through the fog, break through the facade
dissolve all the walls just let em all fall
shake off the chains till they all fall away
fell the lotus unfold inside the ribcage

clear all fear sweep dust from the road
feel the light shine bright inside the temple
smash all thoughts and philosophy
returning to the essence and you set yourself free

POINT OF INFLECTION

I
Refraction
of light
reveals

the oncoming traffic, headlights
piercing like a meteor shower.
falling stars, an endless trail
blinding liquid eyes.

Tonight the freeway is
clogged with traffic,
the endless streams of cars,
the masses of bodies.

The bodies.

Her body.

The vast concentration of
light and life cradled by valley.

She misses her exit.

The fireflies; she remembers the
fireflies in her
backyard they swarmed
like this.

The Poetry of Yoga

Kathy Kottaras

II

She catches the moments in time;
butterflies in a net,
a wave stopped tall in a photograph.
She dives into a thought as though the
depths
of the Pacific are shallow and pale.
With fearlessness
she fills her breath,
she exhales.
She stuns with her visions.

III

The rhythms pound
a hum, a content hum, a solid stoic hum.
The candles dance
mosaic light sizzles in time.
and those long fingers
work on that bass,
hip in line,
laughter cracking simultaneously, with
matches lit, with
curious curving notes.
Some strain to hear it.
She follows the faithful line
of streetlights
wide awake.

IV

spin
circles circles

Yo-yo 'round the world

The world stands in
stillness
with the calm of the
beating heart.
My heart
pounds
in rhythm,

a drum
in synchronization
with
the circles
of the universe

for you.

WINTER LEFT WHEN I WASN'T LOOKING

Winter left when I wasn't looking.
It packed-up in the middle of the night,
And stole silently away
Like a secret lover who slips from the bed sheets at dawn,
Unheard, but somehow still felt.

It quietly lifted its icy fingers from my back,
Disappeared down the storm drain,
Melted into the tulip bed,
Evaporated in the March wind.

Just when I had resigned myself to its inevitability,
Accepted the need to wear the extra layers,
Stopped fighting with the woodpile,
And became accustomed to the daily chill.
Just when I stopped thinking "Winter,"
It slipped out leaving no forwarding address,
No thank you note, no business card.

Elisa Cobb

Traces remain.
Deep puddles,
Soft smell of spring dirt,
Trickling streams down road shoulders,
Empty sleds resting on brown-green hillsides,
And that single glove that
Fell out of the car between snow storms.

But somehow I yawned, gave in, fell asleep
And woke up to another season,
Wondering how I could have missed the departure
Of something I complained about so frequently.

And then I wondered about other things
That passed away like winter.
Parts of myself, old beliefs, stressors that I couldn't change,
Once accepted... once validated as my reality,
Also melted away,
Like turning around to speak
To someone no longer standing there,
Leaving only a trace of conversation hanging in the air.

Elisa Cobb

WEIGHTED

An Ant
And, not a big one.
One of those miniscule creatures,
Falsely insignificant.

Respectfully,
Because of its weighted importance,
Carries the thin bulk
Of a red, papery leaf,
Almost transparent,
And four times his size.

Like a sail on a tiny ship,
Tossed and tugged unpredictably
To and fro;
The skill of toting impossibility
With determination.

Not warrior-like.
More like a construction worker.
Practically putting the heavier and lighter parts
Together
To create a whole yet unknown.

Never before seen.
Yet genetically remembered.
This cancer inside my body,
Like that torn corner of dry leaf,
Borne in my mandibles,
Over my back,
Across my shoulders,
Is difficult to balance
With the rest of me.

The ant carries his burden
Or treasure
Intentionally repeatedly
Over the edge of a concrete step
Miles high.

Then, in doubt,
Back up over that edge
To neutral territory.
Wanders, wondering.
Then tries the same edge again.
And again.
Eventually bravely going all the way
To show me what is possible.

EAGLE LICE

A few years ago a local falconer, Martin Tyner, came to give our class a demonstration. It was thrilling. Martin unwrapped these huge cages with covers like presents and one by one extracted a falcon, a hawk, an owl. They were magnificent creatures, but I had eyes only for Bud, the gorgeous golden eagle with the fierce yellow eyes, who spent most of the lecture perched on Martin's arm.

Martin told us an amazing story about another golden eagle he had rehabbed. Martin told us that when he'd first found him, he'd had a badly injured wing; without the ability to hunt, this beautiful, beautiful creature would soon be dead. The eagle required very delicate, precarious surgery; so delicate, in fact, that he couldn't be sedated and restrained as with a normal operation. Martin would have to hold the injured bird just so for several hours while the veterinarian operated. As he was holding it, a very, very large eagle louse— we're talking about a half-inch long!—climbed out from the bird's feathers and began to crawl up Martin's arm, up his neck, and into his scalp right near his ear.

Martin couldn't risk letting go of the bird to flick the vermin away; the eagle's life was at stake. He had no choice but to stand there, stock still, while this

creepy, disgusting thing probed his scalp.

This was a huge epiphany for me: when you're going through a hard time, you've got to learn to hold onto what's precious no matter what.

Hold it lightly, hold it gently—just hold it. Everything else that's going on—whether it's creepy, or disgusting or annoying or scary—is just eagle lice.

What are your priorities? The louse doesn't want you; it wants the eagle's feathers, so it's not going to stay with you. What is most important here?

What connects you to your Spirit?

The precious being of the eagle was what was important to Martin. For me, my connection to my Spirit, my pipe, my work; that's my eagle, so I've got to protect it no matter what crises are slapping me around.

Wherever there are eagles, there are going to be eagle lice. There's no way around it. Anytime I have a setback, I remind myself, "This is just eagle lice. Just hold that eagle steady so that it will be able to fly once again."

FOR YOU

TIME

The second hand stopped running
Even clocks need to rest

Weighed down and exhausted
From holding
So many moments

The Poetry
of Yoga

Dave Stringer

CHECKING THE ARITHMETIC

if life were a cool calculation
where all of the numbers compute,
then one could sum all of creation
and reduce it all down to the root.
but my mind is a multiplication
of chance and illusion and doubt;
I'm confused and impatient,
a fool at foundation.
I never will figure it out.

am I just a mutation with a curious urge?
an endless vexation, a mistake that recurs?
a singular statistic, a product of the dice?
checking the arithmetic, it's not quite right...

I questioned a mathematician:
my life is uncertain and strange,
tell me what of the human condition
can the priesthood of science explain?
she said, "life is a state of transition,
a pattern of chaos and change;
of loss and division
and love insufficient
to answer the problem of pain."

The Poetry of Yoga

Dave Stringer

am I just a tangle of jumping nerves
or a point on a line describing a curve
flickering in physics' cinema of sight?
checking the arithmetic and it's not quite right...

if I only know what I am feeling
and can't prove the world outside,
then standing or kneeling
or staring at the ceiling
you've gotta have faith as your guide.
the world of sensation
is a puzzling equation,
a persistent hallucination
so you've gotta have faith as your eye...

am I just an ache in a painful world
dreaming awake in a reciprocal blur?
i'm baffled beyond logic and searching for insight,
checking the arithmetic, it's not quite right....

The Poetry of Yoga

Dave Stringer

AT MY WINDOW

illumined and blind,
I dream untroubled
watching my mind.
a stream of bubbles
endlessly rise,
forming, breaking,
ascending the skies
as I awaken

at my window, in my chair,
to watch the clouds go by.
to sit and ponder
a mind that wonders
why it wonders why.

at my window, anywhere
in the world I go
I'm in the best seat.
no view is complete,
but it's the only view I know.

I focus my eyes
where the mirror of sea
and the prism of sky
draw a thin blue line
across the horizon
to vanish in me
at my window
on the grand design

what gives me sight?
and who is seeing
the radiant delight
that thrills my being?

the camera lies
with filtered lenses.
the truth in disguise,
I'm not my senses.

at my window I stare,
but do I really see?
my pained projections
and vain reflections
distort reality.

at my window I'm aware
I'll never really know.
my mind is reeling.
I've got a feeling
it's all a picture show.

connecting the dots
that appear on the screen,
exposing the plot
in the evidence,
selecting the shots
and composing a scene
at my window
of experience.

replay, eyes closed,
talking to myself again.
the only thing I know
is I am.

and all that I see,
all I feel, all I think
will be gone in a glimmer
of dark and light.
a flash that arrives
and dissolves in a blink
at my window
on the infinite.

EMPIRICAL

My body as my laboratory
An inner revolution
elevating chemistry.
Peptides calibrating,
fascia unwinding.
Alchemy on the mat.
Years ago,
the Observer
stirred and stretched.

My life as my laboratory
Tools and scientist evolving.
Enhancing signal.
Redefining, titrating, exploring.
Transforming into a vessel,
more than the physical.
My circuitry like the frog heart,
calmed by the wandering nerve
that tunes me to others.

Embodying the process.
No longer driven to results.
Being result.

WHEN I SHOULD BE MAKING MASTERPIECES

Is there some sort of instruction manual,
a how-to for being an artist when uninspired?
It seems that I suffer from a basic lack of discipline.
Not to mention lack of sleep.
And a recurring headache on just the right side of my head.
Why the right side?
Because my creativity has been dormant these
last three years?
Because the left side of my body is gnarled up and
congealed in places?
Usually I can sleep it off, like most people do
with a hangover.

Oh this endless stream of better-thans and not-as-good-as
my dull insipid vice of comparison
the blemishes on my décolletage
(don't touch them! I can't help it)

I wish to wander, for indeed I am lost.
And fill my days with idle tasks.
When I should be making masterpieces.

The Poetry of Yoga

Lila Donnolo

The skin around my eyes is starting to go.
Hopefully it will reveal that I've smiled
for the second half of my life.
And by the time I'm fifty
and get the face I deserve
all shall see my luminosity.
Each line comes forth so reluctantly.
I have to trick it,
by doing something else.

I'd rather be writing love letters.
And I shall, after my quota is finished.
For once, I can show a little restraint.

Why should I restrain myself?

I long to be Rumi's child: crazy, reckless, and wild
I won't let love and God escape me
I will fantasize with abandon
I will say yes, over and over
I will take risks and use hyperbolic words
I will dare to speak of Destiny and Synchronicity!
I will yell with pleasure and soak their shoulders
with my tears!

I shall make myself a barefoot life, and various things
will stick to my undersides.
You shall hardly know me from your living room.

The Poetry
of Yoga

Eric Shaw

A THOUGHT
OF JESSICA

Uno
Packed with vegetables, a
turkey slow-cooks
in its 250-degree room.
There's a cool bottle of wine
part-drunk
with its steel-hued label.
2 Glasses sit half-full on the
windowsill.

Your long copper hairs
occur to me.

From Arizona
14 years ago
I went to El Paso, Juarez,
and Cobre Canyon
on the night train with old
friends.

No moon.
No seat lights.
The train headlight poured
a yellow landscape
into black.
Little kids in the town had
sandals carved from tires
with a speedy
ultra-marathoner called "El
Caballo Blanco"
we hiked toward gray-rock
hot-tubs on a canyon trail.

Dos
Before the 50s
Americans could say they'd
never entered planes.
except mostly war guys.
We're all sky-shipped to
Mexico and Cape Town

and Moscow now.
You're the vet, senorita.
Crossing over skies with a
scientist's eye

and a great silhouette.
Jessica means "to behold"
some blue website says.
You there, in a silver
fuselage with the flying
fraternity.
Burning jet fuel.

Adding bonus miles.
Watching films?
Buying drinks?
Pressed with delight?

BEFORE NEW YEAR'S

Tres
I've said it before
but you, turbulent with laughter
in that yoga class

tumbled me into blue.
You, there!
Leaping over this proud nation
while laboring,
living in a little boat at home.

Cuatro
Seven days
pressed between holidays.
The first day you're gone,
lightning strikes twice.
My well-poised companion
asks "What?"
Young adventurers have been
lured from town by blood ties.
It's a quieter, roomier town,
post-Xmas.
Parking spaces lie
immodestly open.
Traffic strolls.
Quiet skies are face-to-face with
streets.

A friend drops by with Cabernet
and wrestles me to the couch.

As culture collapses, nature
steps in.
A little walk outside, and I feel
everything.

Cinco
You talk in the lobby
I leave you and find seats.
We spring into the New Year
reckless and lean.

NO CLUE

While the old world
seems to be dying
I look around
Searching for clues
But I find myself
Watching my bare-feet
Hearing the chit-chat
Of a common day

ONE CLUE

Maybe I am here

To watch the wooden floor

While birds scream

Knowing of

Tonight's moon

THIS I KNOW

You are amongst

the luckiest

pausing to breathe

and witness

The Poetry of Yoga

Erika Lukas

ENOUGH | FOR NOW

Last winter I checked out.
I was gone.
Grief so deep I couldn't find it, feel it, express it.
Sponge-like, sucking my emotions
dry during those cold months.

I went through the motions of my days.
Downward dog,
Pigeon,
Warrior,
Even crow.
Breathing the Ujjayi breath.
Bringing air far down to where my heart lay bound.

I was checked out. Gone.
Didn't accomplish anything.
Hard to get things done when you're not there.

And then finally, a last straw.
Another loss.

I screamed-cried-yelled,
in the house by myself.
One long hour.

Then I breathed,
Ujjayi, the victorious breath.

Days later, miles away, I fell alone to the sand
on a beach, couldn't go on.
Ocean winds tracking tears on my cheek.
Drained at last.

Present.
The opening up is so incremental,
the intensity of each minute change
enough for the time being.
All I can handle.

The Poetry of Yoga

Erika Lukas

Spring.
The bulbs came up.
Nothing really has ended,
it just changes, grows,
as I do too.
A psychic tells me to wait.
"Heal Mama."
That I have to grow before the things
I want will come to me.
That there is love and acceptance crossing over.
That I need to trust.

"What am I supposed to become?
How am I supposed to be?
And please, tell me, how do I wait?"

"Put the ashes of your fears onto the water," she
said.
Let them wash away.

But I am afraid to do it.
Right now,
it is more than I can handle.

I used to be able to write funny stuff.
But I can't anymore.
Everything seems too important now,
too much risk if I don't attend to the things
which my heart is opening to.

So I go through my days.
Downward dog,
Warrior
(having given up on crow lately).

And I breathe, Ujjayi, the victorious breath.
Checking in.
For the time being, this is enough for me.

The Poetry of Yoga
Edvige Giunta

PALM SALUTATION

The palm trees she speaks of are the slender, flexible trees
lining Miami, where my daughter was born.

They flex, bend, and survive hurricanes.

I think of another palm tree, the one with a huge, scarred trunk,
its branches framing the collapsed roof of the old house in the garden.
Some forty years ago my mother took the baby tree out of a clay pot,
dug a hole. It grew strong.

I bend left, right, stretch one way, the other, forward now, entwine hands.
I want to be one of those trees, resilient and vulnerable,
with roots no one can dig out.

HALF MOON

The moon makes me think of her, gone for over thirty years.
The crescent moon pinned on the green sweater.
Tonight, it's a small group.
We ask questions.
She guides us through variations of half moon.
Create a wider foundation, foot inward, block farther away.
One side, the other, we balance on one leg,
one hand, stretching the other arm up, an arrow.
Next, feel your core, the wall behind, and if you don't tremble,
don't buckle, only then lift the hand,
place it on your heart,
and stand on that one leg,
feeling the quiet of poetry.

The Poetry of Yoga

Nancy Minges

ALLOWING

Navigating
This tender moment of now.
This breath is enough.
This breath...
Giving rise to this increment of movement;
The owning & releasing
of each grain of sand.
Again & Again
Letting Go
of needing any of it to be different.
Slowing Down
Slowing Down
Slowing Down Some More
Allowing all of it to be held with breath
Resting in Deep Acceptance
...in Deep Trust....
....in Deep Unknowing....
Resting in the undercurrents
of being delightfully tickled
by the equanimity that supports us all.
ALL.
Enlightenment defined
As an intimacy with all things.

The Poetry of Yoga

Nancy Minges

LANDING

No...
Not a stuck place
or knot.
Not a problem spot
or adhesion.
Not an issue
needing release.
No. None of that.
Your experience waits for you.
A perfectly ripening peach
on the tree
growing sweeter day by day.
A tender re-union, waiting.
RELEASE
your need to heal,
your need to awaken.
Simply receive what waits
inside your body.
There IS
Nowhere else to go.
Juicy, Ripe, & Sweet
Your Buddha-Peach Nature.
Just Land.

Sinéad Wallace

7 DAYS ALONE WITH ME

More alone in the chatter and in the traffic
than alone on my cushion.

More questions now because of that answer:
Life is simple when there is only love.

So onward and inward I say in jest,
as though to suggest there might be somewhere else to go.
Where do I go?
When the answer is home. And home is inside,
then I'm already here, so there's nowhere to hide in the world.

I bow to the internal flame
and teachers around me, though i was
not lost I feel that I've found me,
alone on that cushion in the womb of the hills.
Through a blur of goodbye, traffic & noise,
to the prospect of travel, peace, and joys.

A new place. Alone again, really for just a few days.
To be me and feel me and remold the space,
where others can come in to share in this grace.

WHY BIG GIRLS LOVE YOGA

I am big
Round hips jangling like jelly big
Soft arms long like oak branches big
Body birthing spreading hips deep like valleys big

I am big g g g

g g g g g

And like breath, savored and precious
I expand and circulate my mind
Extending my branches
Fertilizing my valleys
With the light from the sun
who cares not how big I think I may be
'cuz to it

I am infinite

The Poetry of Yoga

Seane Corn

COMMUNION

To the living lay dying, whispers, secrets and longing,
of a body sucked bone dry.
You wither in flesh; the moisture wicked, curling into yourself.
Eyes searching, you question spirit, choices, a life lived regretfully.
You blast God, again and again. I let you.
Not long for this life, nor prepared for that which waits.
Any moment now, breathe, any moment, breathe please. Please.
In pain you cry, cry, cry lost, lonely, soul bereft,
hoping that someone will remember you,
see you, behold you as you were.
Awake and glistening, sun soaked warrior,
vibrant, blood pumping, crimson spirit.
Remember me, you plead.
Know me, that beneath the grief, in the time before despair,
life was promise.
Yes, I remember.
You knew I saw past you, through you,
to the you of light and essence,
and I honored and adored you well.
Your pounding heart beat, massive consciousness,
brilliant and alive.
Breathe still. Be still.
You forgot who you are.
Your pain cloaked your newness, rawness, abstract wanting.
Wanting, you lied. Waiting, you died.

Oh God, I pray, do you get it now?
Are you present, in awe, bowed and humbled
to the Grace
we discussed time and again in your bed, me,
no longer tiny,
pressed against your broken, yellowed skin,
smelled like urine,
smelled like love.
Did it happen?
Do you see thru the veil, the emptiness, the anger,
like we talked about?
Did tenderness erupt through your ash,
bone, and nothingness?

Do you look back on your life mystified,
everything lit, exposed, defined and ripe?
Oh the beauty, the grace, the miracle of being, the per-
fection,
the fucking wonder of it all!
God. I saw you once, you know.
Fully, truly.
Shrouded in joy you smiled, body of Christ
on your tongue,
mine, His.
Confessions heard all around.

COMMUNION

The Poetry of Yoga

Seane Corn

Soul companion, spirit guide, Daughter.
Children surrounded us joyfully, unaware they reflect your life,
celebrate your death, they ran around us in a wild,
chaotic circle.
A continuum not lost on anyone.
Just life, you said, then smiled and sighed, we locked eyes,
birthed surrender, and let each other go.
Last rights, you were blessed. Last breath, you went home.

Holy.
God awakens all and holds blessed those who
can't see the light
in the wanting, the waiting, the disappointment, the shame.
You are now All, I told you so.
Heaven, you. Earth, you. Me, you.
Rich in knowing, it's all yours now, the universe,
it's mysteries and magic,
all yours. Magician. Priest. Seer. Teacher.
Soul lit by the spark, the flame, the fire.
Empower me, teach me, show me now, now that you know.
Father you are ignited, blind me.
Father you are sacred, find me.
Father you are awakened, guide me.
In death you have learned.
In God you have merged.
In love you have returned.
Holy.

Ellen McGrath Smith

FORWARD BEND
(PASCHIMOTTANASANA)

I surrender to an avalanche of paper woes,
fold like paper, head aspiring to the toes.

I surrender to the days and nights of solitude,
my rib cage on my thighs a nude
in charcoal, crude initial, husk, a shell.

I surrender to those who do not wish me well,
to those who would stand on my wide, open back.

My east surrenders to my west... sun is setting,
houses, faces, facts forgotten;
the day dissolves into skin-creases.
Chin against the shin long razor-bone;
breasts on kneecap rain clouds, stones.

I surrender to the time the body measures
and the time that measured breath refers to
far beyond the body.

My north and my south
have never known each other's worth;
I fold the map to find the moment's true location.

The Poetry
of Yoga

J.P. McClellan

MEDITATION

Changing Everything
A feather of silence falls
Disturbing Nothing

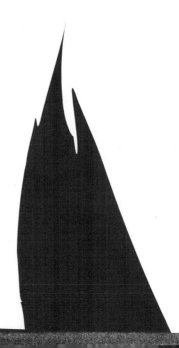

DOUBLE MIRROR DOOR

Wherever I go, there you are.
I see your eyes everywhere I look.
Whenever I touch you,
Fingertip-eyes peer right in,
Piercing skin.
Whenever you look at me, reach out,
Interlace fingers, I cannot tell apart
Your fingers from mine.
Looking at me,
I feel your heart-eyes looking right in,
Touching deep layers of me until
I can no longer tell the difference
Between your heart reaching through me
And my eyes touching your heart.

The Poetry of Yoga

Laurie Blair

My body creeeeeaks
cracks
pockets of releassssssse
(breathe)
(being slowly moving into twisted pose)
calling, calm, centering being
body gliding
hands in prayer
twist (physical twist with word)
(breathe)
(slowly moving to another pose with a twist)
Bubbles occupy my muscles
expanding, popping with each twist and release
wishing release for our mother
suffering under the weight of us
we have lost our way
forgive us
breathe (breathe)
create space
(breathe)
(slowly move to another pose)
Transport to
land of no words
body
heart
mind
soul
merge
e-merges
love
radiating outward
inward
the toughest love to practice is
love of self

(BREATHE)

Laurie Blair

so quick to shift to blame, judgment, punishment.
(breathe)
(slowly move to tree pose)
A dose of gentleness
heals
grounds
erase self
consciousness remains
witnessing this moment
deeply connected
to every thing.
(breathe)
(slowly moving into twisted pose)
Energy flowing
riding through, on, near fear
body gliding
hands in prayer
twist (physical twist with word)
(breathe)
(slowly moving back to mountain)
Form drops away
chakras shining
body gliding
pose to pose
a love affair
with body
with practice
with yoga
calling one to shed ego
disengage from identity
embrace infinity
yoga
body
spirit.
(breathe)

The Poetry of Yoga

Amanda Flores

Concentric circles and the details of clouds.
The robe of an ascetic
and a childhood painting.

Invocation, Resurrection, Resolution
and Primary colors.

This is a beehive,
the words are the hungry bees themselves
mining the ichor
from the minutes
those open pores of the bodies of days.

The flesh formed from the poetry of rhythm,
The eyes,
cracked eggs leaking yellow
yolk.

WITNESS

These are notes.
A telescope to minutiae.

Eggs on the frying pan;
A whiskey slap without the whiskey.

This is a slow, full-footed walk;
the blue Himalayan sky,
The ghost of the Ganga sanctified and polluted.

A portrait of self
and so-called "other;"
a reconciliation of Either/Or.

Day to day to dissection
of dingy dogmas.

No, not propaganda
of the ideal, scripted, Fear-mongering mind;
But a solar powered Festival of lights.

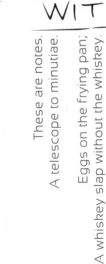

MY GUARD

There is a suffering that will come without my guard.
My guard is this moment.
This moment, this moment, my mantra, and I love my guard.
My puppy is adoring me with his eyes.
My spring flowers are coming up to bloom.
The sun playfully peeks at me through the clouds.
Hello, sun, nice to see you again.
Always the guard whispers in my ear, this moment, this moment, this moment, this moment.
My grand-son squeezes my neck with his tiny skinny arms...
Nana, Nana, I love you.
My husband whispers in my ear, I am always here for you.
Always the guard whispering in my ear, this moment, this moment.
My son says, "I want to die." That was that moment.
That moment was that moment.
My guard says this moment, this moment.
This moment my son is alive.
My heart swells with love and gratitude for my guard,
this moment, this moment, this moment.

THE CRICKETS' MEDITATION

When crickets sing, they sing for the moon
That loyal spectator, spilling light upon their stage

Crickets sing to collaborate with
The wind's breath
To accompany the caterpillar
In metamorphosis
The butterfly's first flight

When crickets sing, they sing for
Cockroaches in the world of Raid spray
The circus lion's silenced roar
The Beta fish
That fights his own reflection

Crickets sing to honor all living things
Even the mosquito that buzzes
And bites

When crickets sing, they break the barriers
We've built around our hearts
With the tools we've gathered for protection
They clear the junk drawers of our minds

Crickets sing to move
Invisible walls of silence
Thick forests of resistance
To connect every beating heart

When crickets sing they echo
Thich Nhat Hanh:
Open your eyes to the clouds
The flowers
The life within life

Crickets sing for the beauty
Not of what was, or what will be
But of what is
For those still looking for their wings

Crickets sing for dreams stitched in the night sky
Held together by glue of starlight

When crickets sing, they sing to love the questions
Which have no answers
And release them to the night sky

COURAGE

Golden light streams
Into the garden studio
I sit cross-legged
In the center of my mat
Forearms rest on knees
Palms turned up
Ready to receive
The moment
Courage is showing up for practice,
The teacher says
I sit up straighter
Spine lengthens
Chin rises
Fingers uncurl
To create bowls
The teacher invites us
To raise our palms
In prayer position
Touch foreheads
Faces
Chests

SERVING LIFE

my life sentence
is a question
the answer
is yes

The Poetry of Yoga

Naima Penniman

DROP OF WATER

the stars have spent lifetimes
trying to reach us with the message
that our light can inspire solar systems if we let it
shine like the moon's reflection
of her suns and daughters
great great great grandmothers and fathers
foretold this time of great blessing and slaughter
when we'd decide between drought
and drowning in water

or rising like mist from toxic streams
with dreams of becoming rainwater
and falling pure to the earth to quench
the thirst we'd forgotten
was the reason we struggle in
this web that we're caught in
is not a trap
but an intricate pattern
like a labyrinth, a snowflake
or crystal of water

or the concentric rings of a tree
that still makes a sound
long after it's fallen
in a forest that lived
even if no one saw it
and fed the world its breath
whether or not we applauded
one hand clapping sounds a lot like
the rhythm we lost in
generations who sang
even as they departed

we paved concrete
over the pores of the earth
to make our lives harder
and built buildings to scrape skies
trying to get closer to God
but moved farther

The Poetry of Yoga

Naima Penniman

from the source that birthed
the first light in the darkness
we stole from our mother
and we continue to rob her
for diamonds and gold
and our ancestors' bones
disappeared from their coffins

turned hollow
so they could fly
with the weight of the fodder
on her wings she has
dust inside her brain
and got caught up
thinking pain was her fate
but this is what you said
that you wanted

whether we knew it or not
the universe responded
to every vision and image
and nightmare we've thought of
our words are like bullets
and we call the shots
by their names
and they come running
with gifts in their pockets

impressions of lessons of
the stories
life taught us
that our dreams are impossible
so we keep them in closets
and now we stand
at the doorway
in the hallway
life brought us

to this cross roads
of lost hope and undeniable
promise

where we choose between paths
beyond rightness or wrongness
that will lead to the brink
of the planet's exhaustion
or the age of compassion
where the meek become strongest
and reinherit the earth
and redefine progress

so don't be scared of the spark
in the spell of great darkness
or afraid of the light
in the moment of dawning
or the heights you will reach
when you rise to your calling
and release all your rain
call it flying
or falling

let go of your wanting
and give into your longing
to live free of possessions
and full of belonging
to the intricate infinite
we're all a part of
the web that you wove
in a dream you'd forgotten
was the Creator awaking
into your conscious
condensation of vapor
into a droplet of water

The Poetry
of Yoga

Naima Penniman

BEING HUMAN

I wonder if the sun debates dawn
some mornings
not wanting to rise
out of bed
from under the down-feather horizon

if the sky grows tired
of being everywhere at once
adapting to the mood swings of the weather

if the clouds drift off
trying to hold themselves together
make deals with gravity
to loiter a little longer

I wonder if rain is scared
of falling
if it has trouble letting go

if snow flakes get sick
of being perfect all the time
each one trying to be one-of-a-kind

I wonder if stars wish
upon themselves before they die
if they need to teach their young how to shine

I wonder if shadows long
to just for once feel the sun
if they get lost in the shuffle
not knowing where they're from

I wonder if sunrise and sunset
respect each other
even though they've never met
if volcanoes get stressed
if storms have regrets
if compost believes in life after death
I wonder if breath ever thinks
about suicide
I wonder if the wind just wants to sit
still sometimes
and watch the world pass by

if smoke was born knowing how to rise
if rainbows get shy back stage
not sure if their colors match right

I wonder if lightning sets an alarm clock
to know when to crack
if rivers ever stop
and think of turning back

if streams meet the wrong sea
and their whole lives run off-track
I wonder if the snow wants to be black

if the soil thinks she's too dark
if butterflies want to cover up their marks
if rocks are self-conscious of their weight
if mountains are insecure of their strength

I wonder if waves get discouraged
crawling up the sand
only to be pulled back again

to where they began

I wonder if land feels stepped upon
if sand feels insignificant
if trees need to question their lovers
to know where they stand

if branches waver in the crossroads
unsure of which way to grow
if the leaves understand they're replaceable
and still dance when the wind blows

I wonder where the moon goes
when she is hiding
I want to find her there
and watch the ocean
spin from a distance

listen to her
stir in her sleep
effort give way to existence

The Poetry of Yoga

Beandrea July

FOREST HAIKU

When I stop and sit
among the redwoods praying
abundance is real

CHAKRA BILL OF RIGHTS

First,
Smelling roots, I have the right to exist.

Second,
Tasting water, I have the right to change and to create.

Third,
Seeing with eyes,

I have the right to actualize myself in the world.

Fourth,
Touching with heart, I have the right to feel.

Fifth,
Hearing with ears, I have the right to speak Truth.

Sixth,
Guided by Intuition, I have the right to envision.

Seventh,
Knowing a Higher Self, I have the right to transcend duality.

SPINE

As brain floats on clouds where
head meets neck between
shoulder blades as tailbone
plugs in
Spine
channels Light
up from Earth
as beauty waterfalls over cliffs
of bone
and waves of flesh and fluid
mirror the tides
Inside this motion
while sitting still
I know.
I am.
Divine.

Jemma King

THROUGH THE SEVEN

In Asanas
my shoeless mind
waits patiently
for the bolt's dissolve
and alchemy.

Its prismatic self leaps
loose from the crown,
hitchhikes on the breath
under violet brows and throat.

Here, below the 49th
octave, the world's story
made hieroglyphic, in red
cell and bone.

I am tracing the
outside curve
of muscle, a deathbed
of two dozen vermillion
petals.

My consciousness is
a wandering thing,
a franchise of neurons
unlocked
and growing.
The crescent moon is
waxing full,

unhooks me
from Samsara.

TEMPLE

I was fifteen when
They cut my life apart with knives.

First time my mother said she'd buy me a necklace
to hide the scar
They never told about the side-effects of that surgery
of dried-out hands
that could no longer sweat
Plates slipped and broke
A blurred sensation now where touch
and texture once gave joy

Next year a bigger scar
left and right across this young belly
"Had to do that... in case of gangrene
We take out nerve ganglions - five of them
on either side of the spine."

I woke up bloated and bewildered
"Ginger-beer helps," a nurse offered.

Two sweet boys came to visit with a crate full
But I was lost
something gone

Feet dried out
and slid from under
Skin cracked and bled I walked on knives
wore socks in summer

later learned that also gone
was any chance to conceive a child.

Head
Heart
Belly now were living separate lives
Fear filled in the spaces

Heart rose and crashed
Love passed by unspoken
Sex loomed and left
Head hung on
Clinging to ideas, ideals
"Must stay above it all."

Half my life seemed stolen
Body shrank as all sense of being, feeling
Clung to bone
The loss got quickly buried

Survival came with work and study
'til twelve years on
Yoga found me
was the band-aid
gave me strength and power
a practice hard enough to fortify my walls
we are miracles of 'repair work'

so long as no one digs into our psyche!

Then one day the bubble burst
And there I was inside still hiding

Fame and struggle had blinded me to a
simple realization
"There must be another way."

Across India up and down
I traveled searching for a teacher
Who could show me how
And where the secret lay.

Great myths are not so simple...
they answer prayers another way.
A voice spoke up from deep inside
And lead me to a place called Karnak
Where each day the sun rose from the sea
And on the temple walls
Lovely deities carved in stone
Sang, danced in ecstasy, played flute
The morning sun upon them.

No stern church with pointed spire
Or sermons preached... cerebral dams
No thin and bony nuns or skin-tight yogis here
Voluptuous femininity brought stone to life.

I stood in silence
Awakening slowly to unravel
And recover a sacred, sensual truth

The Poetry of Yoga

Angela Farmer

Round breasts, full buttocks, bellies
curving swaying
to unheard music
Faces lifted to a lover's kiss
the first long shafts of sunlight
breaking loose.

I saw the path that I had followed
stern and thin - onwards leading upwards
I saw myself alone
a yogi in a cave
I saw how every curve and roundness
sense of touch and joy
had been denied
softness traded for hard lines of something
called perfection
A path of man so straight and narrow...

Something shifted then
fell, let go
sweet memories returning
The sun's warm rays had touched me deep
and lovingly

It was a moment in my life
of change
conception of a woman's path

A way to own this body
Filling it with
me
with huge forgiveness and delight.

THE WEB

Let me spin you a story of rainbows and wishes,
and angels and faeries with earth saving missions.
A story of people from faraway places
who believe that the weaver is mother of creation.

A people that build their houses of clay.
Whose tradition is to speak to the land when they pray.
Painted houses shine bright in the desert.
Creativity is free,
Whether you are pauper or president.

Remembering times when tradition was passed down
from mother to daughter.
When the community came to the center for solace.
Where houses are round because corners are sharp.

Where buildings breathe like we do!

Cut! Now it is two thousand and nine.
Janine Benyus tells us that bio-mimicry has reached its time.
Build like the ancients and make products like webs.
Forget about dams and build Permaculture swales instead.

The Poetry of Yoga

Erin Alexander

As we re-member, society can thrive.
And the people will say thank god we're alive.
Because to live in concrete boxes and
breathe in toxic fumes,
has left us with way too many problems to consume.

Thank god we have answers taken from the past.
From the people who believed that there is spirit in the land.
Give honor to the ancestors like Chief Seattle
and of course William Morris.

They taught us to see sustainability as progress.

The concept of creation and innovation is simple.
Take only what you need and leave some for the rest of us.
In the windows of the web there are
thousands of possibilities.
The task is to find the right light and illuminate the entry.

MEDITATION FOR A PEBBLE

The ocean rocks you, little by little, up onto a beach whose
rippling sand looks like fine powdered saffron streaking
crushed diamonds.

The gentle sun dries you, warms you.
You sigh with relief. At last, you are still. The waves recede.
They are on their own journey. Seagulls flap past.
They trill mournfully to one another. Yet, they embody joy.
They fly off, towards the sun.

You are alone again.
This time, your solitude feels
companionable.

You are a pebble. Your own weight brings you comfort.
Yes, you can be thrown, turned, tossed.
But you can also be held.

You are dove-gray, worn more on one side than on the other.
A pure white stripe hugs your cool center, like a belt that has
no buckle. This stripe sets you apart, adding charm.
You look as though an invisible hand painted you.

While you cannot stand up tall, you can lie flat with ease.
You are ease. Seize ease.

Some may say that you are hard. Even you, though, are
soft. The water carried you to this pristine beach, caressing
you, curving around your contours until you surrendered.

Your memories are of mussel clusters and vague echoes,
supple starfish and miniscule pearls.

When a child's hand scoops you up from the sand, your
firm composure comforts the child. She hears your heart.

Your silent modesty invites light that can cast no shadow.
When the child sets you on her altar, you remain the same.
She, however, is changed.

Each morning, the child traces your stripe with her finger.

So you recline. You harbor neither hope nor regret.
You are touched or not touched, revered or not revered.
Words do not hurt you.

The Poetry of Yoga

Effy Redman

You neither seek the sun's heat nor shrink from winter's cold.
If lichen grows across you, you welcome the precious lichen.
When lizards congregate around your perimeter,
you smile at the lizards' congregation.

Perhaps the child slips you into her pocket, to take you for
a walk. And perhaps, along the way, you tumble unnoticed
through a hole in her coat pocket, down to the worn, dusty,
meandering path.

You lie there, smaller than a footprint.

You are not lost, wasted, or forgotten.

New eyes will see you. Loving hands will again cradle you.
Sweet voices will, once more, praise your distinctive stripe.

Later, the crescent moon rises through silver haze,
illuminating you like a star's mirror.
Your narrow stripe glimmers.

A waking owl swoops above you, softly calling, searching.
The sound resonates delicately through you.

You begin to breathe.

DOOR KNOB

Sometimes I feel blocked
A cool fall breeze rustles leaves
The house is empty

The Poetry of Yoga

of Yoga

Olga Alvarado

ANCESTORS

The ashes are our ancestors,
and we are the burning wood.

The smoke is our cost of living,
the impurities
leaving our bodies
as we rise.

MULTITUDE

a thread of binah saturates this universe. colors cascade into shapes and shadows, pungent forms swift in their delivery of elsewhere. the kenya bones, the jamaica bones, the senegal bones, the mali bones, the barbados bones, the haiti bones, the north carolina bones, the black bones, the disappear bones, the solar bones, the earth bones, the mended bones quilt a family, the epic bones hold the beginnings.

browns, yellows, reds, and blues search for a home inside this skin, a blanket of dense multiplicity pulsing in their wake. the substance of things hoped for is made of flesh and migration. the juniper level muscles, the laurinburg muscles, the staten island muscles, the greensboro muscles, the washington, d.c. muscles, the echo muscles, the distance muscles, the jubilee muscles, the mother's hands, the grandma's mouth, the auntie's nose, the people's breath is heavy with prayer, the baby's spine is set to grow.

this palimpsest layers like time. memory reconstructs what truth remembers. even a song survives slavery. the first tongues, the auction block tongues, the plantation tongues, the sharecropper tongues, the sunday service tongues, the mourning tongues, the watermelon tongues, the chicken tongues, the severed tongues, the laughing tongues, the weary tongues, the working tongues, the southeast tongues get stuck on the bus, the gullah tongues get swallowed by the sea.

she is the story we keep on telling. orange, sea green, coral, turquoise, magenta bleed through the lines, trace patterns on the ocean of her process. its multitude weaves the way inside the tide. the why tides and the dry tides, the scar tides and the death tides, the womb tides and the wonder tides, the better tides and the bitter tides, the have tides and the loss tides. the every tides and the never tides. the any tides and the ain't tides. the there tides and the where tides. see how the tide moves on. see how binah blooms more.

TO BE A SILENT
BACKSEAT DRIVER

I surrender myself to the Fate which controls me.
Strapped to the fender of The Cosmic Jalopy,
I release the brakes from my skates as we start,
grasp the rope with both hands for dear life,
and close my eyes as we roll onto the freeway.

Rocks and trees whizz by in a blur.
Passing diesels make my teeth chatter.
Squirrels crossing risk both life and limb,
but, then again, so do I, for
a glance at the wheel shows that there's no one there.

I trust that She's simply transparent,
mime for a honk from a monstrous, black truck,
and hope this thing don't fall apart.

The Poetry of Yoga

Kim Stevens-Redstone

SANSKRIT DREAM

Some dreams are very vivid, and there's some I can't recall,
but last night I dreamed in Sanskrit and understood it all.

Asanas and yamas were floating through my head.
I completely comprehended each word not being said.
Cross-legged Maharishi floating inches from the ground.
I barely even blinked when he gifted me my sound.
Sometimes I'm late for a math test,
running through an endless hall, but last night I dreamed in Sanskrit
and understood it all.

A room full of low sweet sounds drifting softly to my ear,
sinking deep into my brain, and becoming crystal clear.
George Harrison touched the guru and then slowly walked away.
As he passed me on my mat he whispered "Namaste."

The Poetry of Yoga

Kim Stevens-
Redstone

Once I was Debbie Gibson and I was singing in the mall,
but last night I dreamed in Sanskrit and understood it all.
The elephant in the corner held his hands out like a bowl,
saying "Aum Gam Ganapataye Namaha," his words became my soul.
I breathed in Om and breathed out Sah, as I lifted off the floor,
Followed the sound of the mantra as it drifted through the door.

Sometimes I'm on the edge of a cliff, and I wake just as I fall.
Last night I dreamed in Sanskrit.
And understood it.

All.

Matthew McConnell

A WISH

to be vibrant, to be healthy. to speak when the moment strikes. to look forward. to not pause or hesitate or be lost in translation or forgotten in a stale cloud of mediocrity. to accept without resignation. to move beyond the anxiety of doubt or disbelief or lack of faith. to get good sleep. to stretch and breathe... inhale... exhale... giving thanks for this moment and these bodies.

to start this day with loving grace, bless us all and kiss your face. to dance naked in the firelight with a full moon high in the sky shining bright. to love with all that i have, and when it's difficult and needed, more. to lie next to you, beside you, inside of you.

to play. to spin lights and sticks and dance and do simple yet beautiful tricks. to perform, for me and you... i might even show up wearing neon colored clown shoes. to hear the music, even when it stops. to feel the rush of waves. to actively create the connections and ways that will sustain us as we experience darker days, so roll with it.

to be vibrant, healthy. to put one sure foot in front of the other, taking me to where i'm going and arriving with each step.

to dream wide awake, imagining the possibilities while planting flowers in the desert.

to ask. to remember. forget. hold on and let go. to circle the ancient tower and shapeshift.

if i had just one, that'd be my wish.

LIBERTAS

In the darkest times in my life
I have discovered an inner strength and power,
an ability to trust in the forces
that were conspiring to make me real.

At the height of fear I have felt the birth of courage.
When I've been certain that I couldn't endure,
something within miraculously restores me to life,
puts flesh on my bones, and air in my lungs.
"You're not done yet, so rise."

This is how I have become authentic.
I have learned how to surrender,
to accept what I most ardently resist with faith.
I don't know where I will be led,
how I will earn my living,
where I will live or much of anything else.
What I do know is that I can trust in life.
I remember the truth,
I hold the keys to my own freedom.
Hail Libertas!

WHEN GRAVITY SLEEPS

I lay down next to you
Normally beds are for sleeping
But tiredness is waiting
For me hours in the future
The mattress is a white board
For your dreams
As you gently grind your teeth
I snuggle into a warm crevice
Situated in your shoulder blade
It's a canyon cut deep
A wrinkle on your cheek
Reminding me of the trail
We climbed together in Sedona
When gravity sleeps rocks float
and become soft as pillows
An empty mind and a full heart
Remind me why
Beds are not always for sleeping
Sometimes they are simply
For keeping us close
Between two worlds

The Poetry of Yoga

Gopikrishnan
Kottoor

A PAIR OF SLIPPERS

A Pair of slippers
can do no wrong.
But day long
it walks and talks
in a language
its own.
Kills, spills blood
without letting you know
and lets you
walk on
upon flower
and thorn
and at the end of the day
back home
you don't just bother.

you just let it open
at the doorstep
for its sins
for you
it did all day
without remorse
all just for you
to let you be
on your feet
you don't let it
come up with you
you don't take it
in your hands
to pray

The Poetry of Yoga

Gopikrishnan
Kottoor

RADHA-KRISHNA

Don't you,
ever see my tears?

Or is it
that you always see them
and pass through them
like curtain beads?

Did it need you,
beloved,
to tell me
that love is always sadness,

even if your lover
is a
god ?

All day I spread
the bright yellow-red pagoda flowers
on your bed
under the fragrant oleander bloom.

Remember, Krishna,
I told you I would make you
a flower-bed?

I have kept my word.
And now, until you come to see it,
I'll lie beside,

On your
thorns

The Poetry of Yoga

Robbi Nester

NIRALAMBA HALASANA (UNSUPPORTED PLOUGH)

These blades cut deep,
carving out a cave
from legs and torso,
where intestines'
pearly ropes fall free,
and the heart, suspended,
beats its regular tattoo
against the chest until
the vaulted rafters ring.
The lungs two sails
spread their manta wings,
and breath bears me down
through the sweet darkness,
all the way to the end.

The **Poetry** of **Yoga**

Robbi Nester

The moon swells like a seedpod.
Inside the quiet studio, I take
my aching head into my hands,
fingers web to web. A breath,
and then this awkward frame
ascends, becomes an aspen,
flexing in a nonexistent breeze.
Grounded in air, movement merges
with stillness, my ear a vehicle
for surging tides, the galaxies'
faint hum. Everywhere
and nowhere, the worlds
fall away, balanced
on these two arms.

SALAMBA SIRSASANA (HEADSTAND)

The Poetry of Yoga

Robbi Nester

BADDHAKONASANA
(BOUND ANGLE)

These feet have seldom met.
All lifetime long, fated to tread
their single paths on yielding earth,
to press parched soles against
unsympathetic streets, they
desire only new routes, never
dreaming what they truly seek.
Yet arch to arch, each toe
pressing its long-lost opposite,
these feet have met their match.
Bound in a forced embrace, they find
a blessing in this union, welded
in a prayer to all things lost,
to what was always there.

On the road to the studio, the hills
undulate under the clouds like fish
in the shallows, soft morning light
singing on their silver scales.
I want to lie down in that light
and become a hill, but my mind
won't let me. Let me try again
to still the muscles' long
sigh as legs enfold the hips,
tucked under like hospital corners,
the thighs pulled taut as a harp string,
the ribs pried open as I
lie back on the folded blankets
exposing my heart to the world.

SUPTA VIRASANA
(RECLINING HERO)

The Poetry of Yoga

John Schumacher

WELCOME THE NIGHT

Though Night sees you inside your dreams,
No, he's not the stranger that he might seem.
Raise the blinds, read the signs
And let evening come inside.
Please don't hide,
Nght will show the way.

Welcome the Night
Let the Night bring In-Sight
Let the Sight clear the Darkness away.
Be not afraid
Feel the evening pervade
Let the Clear Light of Night in to show you the way.

The Poetry of Yoga

John Schumacher

TU SENS

A voice whispers sounds you fear
The words and ideas you hear
They come from inside, from them you hide
And all you know are tears.

Let go, see what's on your mind
Let go, and you will find
The walls you've made, the prayers you've prayed
Were born to keep you blind.

And then, when you know what it means to see
Your flesh and your spirit hold the key
The locks will all open before your hand
No longer are you in an empty land.

The Poetry
of Yoga

Sonam Gyaltsen

Emotion, love, and heart feelings that express,
passion in a soul without fear.
If this flower truly lasts forever,
the beautiful impermanence is clear.

SOUL

LIFE

I've seen birds dance,
a penguin cry and insects fear.
We are all equally part of this delicate sphere.

The Poetry of Yoga

Temple Symonds

HARMONIUM

I hear the harmonium

The quiet, constant sound of the instrument

Fingers move, slowly, while the other hand gives breath

And the chanting begins

We call out to he who is most divine

And we call out to that place in each of us

Between you and me but

And breathe through the truth that they are one and the same

I have already put you on the other side of the fence and

That we are all one and the same

Deemed you unlike me

There is no difference between him and me

Acknowledged that we are on different paths.

I'm rethinking my position

Questioning everything and nothing and

Breathing through silent answers

Seeking strength without struggle

Once again

On the mat

The Poetry of Yoga

Temple Symonds

I hear the harmonium

I hear the collective consciousness that surrounds me and
Past these bones

I sing
Into the open heart, open spirit

For the girl I wasn't
Into the open

For the one I might never be
I don't go there often;

For the woman I am in this moment
Sometimes the sun hurts my eyes

Bruised, yet
And shows me my battle scars

Open, wild and free
Today I will stand

In this moment
Planted, and

Unafraid
I will sing to the divine

In this moment
I will hear my own voice, yours and countless others

I see my divinity, my right to be loved by him and you and me and all
I will accept my connection

This is my right
And I will breathe into this truth

My obligation to this life, to connect
That there is no difference between the divine and me

And to investigate
That there is no difference between you and me

Past skin receptors and central nervous system

EARTHLY GRACE

Be still for a moment
if you want to know what movement is.

Let go of your body,
As if it belonged to the Earth all along.

Surrender the spine
into gravity's embrace
let her teach you
how before you can grow tall
you must crawl.

Flesh folding into itself
this you shaped package
blood and bones dreaming
this fire from deep within.

Sinking in between the waves
in this ocean of breath
where we pray because life is
this pleasure and this joy.

LET GO

Let go
Let the weight of who you really are
Break through fear, greed, anger
Passing them by like previous fancies
Which no longer amuse you

Let go
Without outstretched arms
Hoping for salvation
Expecting a sense of safety
Or attempting to cushion some imagined impact

Let go
And you will know
You are aimed for
The only destination that you can have

Let go into Life
And you will find out who you are

Let go into Life
The only one you have

The Poetry of Yoga

Lin Ostler

I am not the mighty,
the one they call the setting sun,
nor does Surya rise in me.

I am not the feast,
not the grist nor the loaves.
I am the remnants beneath the grindstone,
the foolscap fomenting poems.

You may not invite me
yet, I am inside the impulse to gather,
to commune among comestibles.

I am not the ballet
but the Yogini teetering on the wire.

I gather stamens & petals
from every bloom, mourn their parching
& scatter the wisps over the waters

before I enter. Otter-like
I dip and swirl beneath them,
emerging dispersed with petals

and I float, eyes to the stars.

I am not the stars, not the sparkler
in an elegant tart, yet I have
startled with nectars.

NOT THE ONE I AM

The Poetry of Yoga

Lin Ostler

I am not the Mother of the Sea, Yemoya,
but her wet nurse.

I listen,
the one whose eyes are closed,
swaying to the rhythms in the room

not the hands on the drum
but the ear to its thrum, foretelling
the juicy maturity of each note.

When fires ravage
I gather the victims and blow ashes
from their eyes, then disappear
when they are lucid.

I am not the fire, the spicy Pitta Vata
but the Kapha, an earthy root.

Sometimes I was the fire
when babies rocketed from my womb,
when my poems were the coal beds
where you ventured with tender, untested soles.

Perhaps you mimicked my movements
until you were folded into your own.

I am the folds in the tapestry,
the uniting force.
I am that.

The Poetry
of Yoga

Purvi Shah

WHY NOT LIVE

in the terrain of dreams? Your lips

are softer there & kisses need not
fly. Rather they may saunter, provide   a pause

and singular seduction: wrap the moment
in honesty & a delight unseen. This is the space

of two people, how a flash of darkness can bring rains
or the daylight to break or expectation itself to surrender,

how a thread you cannot hold can yet last you
a lifetime. You think:

this is all too dreamy for me. I say right on,
write on.

GRIEVING

The wasp has been between the frame
and the screen for four days now.

I approach the sill, watch his legs
creep forward with stilted movements.
There is no plan. His twitching body
no longer holds the screen well
and it meets the sill as his wings fail.

The old window grates stiffly in its track.
One hand braces it; my other stabs a square
in the screen, wires popping with protests.

I have been stung before but still jump
and squeak when he waddles toward me.
I shove the window shut and hope
he's as smart as I want him to be.

Shortly, I force the rattling window open
again and ease a cup over his fragile
form. The plastic grates as I drag it.
Cringing, I start a mantra of please,
don't get crushed expecting his body
to seep under the rim at any moment.

The cup settles around the hole, and I wait.
Soon, he bursts from the window
to the world, his wings working after all.
As I patch the hole with packing tape,
I realize I need to call my mother back,
ask about the funeral arrangements.

The Poetry of Yoga

Prem Mohan
Lakhotia

EXPRESSIONS AND REALIZATION

Not the glamour of metaphors
But the simplicity of expressions
That plays up on the inner ocean
Create the beauty of our lives.

Divinity finds no better home than
In the heart's pure abode of reflection.
They say, a man is what he thinks
And creates what he feels and sees.

Personal realization is my conviction
Six decades of speaking in silence
Have kept me smart and full of service
On the path of life's journey for beauty.

A MOMENT OF ETERNITY

A moment of eternity
In the mortal hours
Has more credence than
All the glamour showers.

To make life a channel of
Pure thoughts and noble deeds
Even for the tiniest time
Is worthier than recorded creeds.

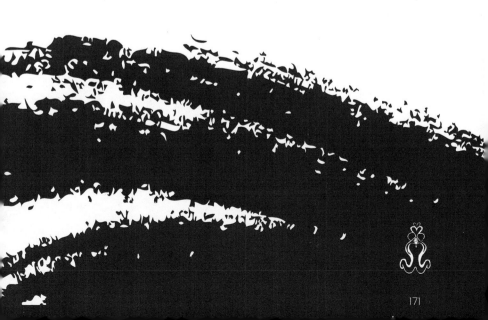

The Poetry of Yoga

Andrea Boyd

I imagine that the only rules a revolution has, are those set by nature.
I imagine that revolution is naked, and doesn't have a dress code,
where "indecent exposure" isn't the blessed bodies we've been given,
but the revealing of what isn't decent, the cruel treatment
of innocent creatures that would rather keep their feet.
Chickens can't be exonerated from death row or march in protest.
The revolution won't have a limit, won't be according to a permit.
What permit do we need to be free? What permit is required that permits one to pay
someone else to kill for a fleeting pleasure on the lips, back, arm, skin?
The permit of human being?
What if we stopped with this word human, and just said being?
Would that help? Or would we still find our treatment of these 'others' permissible?
I imagine revolution to be off the clock of time, no 9 to 5,
but by the rhythms of life, the rhythms of rhyme.
It's okay if you don't like it, don't like me, are afraid,
are appalled by what I say, by what I do.
My goal is not to impress you, but to press upon buttons that might be the alarm.

REVOLUTION

ODE TO YOUR LOVING NATURE

Silky daisies, and lilies, and orchids
caressing the veil of your silvery hair,
like waterfalls from the sky
and resting on the sweetness of your womb.
Mother Nature is waiting for your graceful foot to touch the ground.
You open your measured dance on the whispering grass,
and squirrels and trees rejoice at the melody of your wise steps.
You are floating in space and time,
on the silent wings of a newborn butterfly,
speaking words of kindness to a restless World.
Your eyes are bathed in the fiery light of Life,
and your humane prayers are murmured to the clouds.
You're the Mother of the Sun.
You are precious.
You are Love.

The Poetry of Yoga

DHL CERO

DAY BEFORE | CUAUHNAHUAC

When the win becomes HOW
The disease of competition ties
with creation forever overtime
We are beginning to realize
that we love everyone.

Our hunger is for spiritual waterfalls.
When the birds leave the cages.
When the children put down their ambitions.
When the moms stop controlling
the wild magical babies.
When the air smells like sugar cane
not from burning
but from galactic burps.

When the bowls of cereal taste like clay and the
pizza is made
of Oaxacan cheese
and Congolese tomato seeds.
When the eagle and the condor land on a lost pup-
py, tackling, nipping, and carrying
away to the land of passion.
When the men love the women with sacred eyes.
When the jealous people lie down
and kiss the fallen leaves.
When the flowers are no longer cut.
When the trees are honored as prophets.

The Poetry of Yoga

DHL CERO

When the Cuban prophetess removes
her bandana and transforms
it into a bandage for a bleeding hobo.

When the sky explodes with pure magic.
When the song smashes the face with pure energy,
igniting the love of beans and cheese.

When the vegan dominatrix puts down her voice
and picks up a
quesadilla made by a Mayan princess.

When the anger turns into anger.
When the punches are pulled and
pushed back into
the Earth.

When they arrive.
When they love.
When they love.
When they give in.
When they see it.
We are free.
Free.
Free.
We say. Free!

THIRST IS

Drink this,

moons spin and whirl in the off worlds of the heart.
Such water as I carry is his, by worth, by curve
of smile and horizon.

In dream, he lifted the cup, saying, Drink this,

I tasted the wild sage of Grenada,
fireflies in a veil of evening,
the kissed stones of Mecca.
Monarch butterflies in flight 3 generations,
knowing no origin but desire.

My thirst is that migration, that carried cup, that shiver,
fever, cloud.

He is mirror, door, whisper, fire, husky-tongued moonlight

This thirst is not for quenching,
But for drowning in.

I offer my body's secret body
to the Dark One.

The wind in the piney canyon
is tonight, his voice,
strong and musical, under Lyra and the Scales,
the Lion Rampant.

FOR KNOWING WATER

Drink this,

I do and taste sovereignty
Inside this surrender.

Flickers take wing, over hills, over ridge line,
I follow

crossing thresholds
to his bed,
scent of honeysuckle and wetland.

Judyth says, I listen closely
to the voice of the Beloved.

From the seed of one dropped decibel,
mountains rise,
inside his cadence,
fresh rivers spring.

THIS WILL FIND YOU READY

When you lose everything, then you track.

This world is always spinning,
on chicken legs, at the edge of the forest.
You will need each chip of obsidian, every flake of flint,
all caught parts of conversations,
glimpses of clematis behind fences in hidden courtyards,
to remember a soaker rain, trill of orioles at first light.

Every scent of hyacinth, of jasmine, is a vow,
every bird song, a call to prayer,
a rooftop in another city, but always your own.

Call in all the magic.
Set a place at your table, silver knives, fish bones,
chess pieces of ancient ivory.
Can you see it? You've been so many times.

You've been the one who kneads the bread,
the one who comes to the table in sackcloth,
the one who sits beside the king, in aquamarine and emerald.
The crown, the crow, the crone,
it is all the same.

This time bring the sword,

This blade strikes once and once only.

Ask for leave, and do one thing right,
it's all you can do.
You must ask your question.

Permission will be given in both worlds.
There is a second chance,
at least in this story.

Tell it the old way, aloud.
Build a fire of the nine woods gathered, apple,
hawthorn, hazel, willow, rowan, vine and fir.

You already know. You have done this.

You will make what you desire appear, by your own
seeking,
by your willingness
to sing as you approach,
to walk slowly, to keep going,

to serve what you walk towards with your whole,
broken,
wild heart.

The **Poetry** of **Yoga**

Judyth Hill

WAGE PEACE

Wage peace with your breath.

Breathe in firemen and rubble,
Breathe out whole buildings and flocks of red wing
blackbirds.

Breathe in terrorists
and breathe out sleeping children and freshly mown
fields.

Breathe in confusion and breathe out maple trees.
Breathe in the fallen and breathe out lifelong friend-
ships intact.

The Poetry of Yoga

Judyth Hill

Wage peace with your listening:
hearing sirens, pray loud.
Remember your tools:
flower seeds, clothes pins, clean rivers.
Make soup.
Play music, memorize the words for thank you in
three languages.
Learn to knit, and make a hat.

Think of chaos as dancing raspberries,

imagine grief
as the out breath of beauty
or the gesture of fish.

Swim for the other side.
Wage peace.
Never has the world seemed so fresh and precious.

Have a cup of tea and rejoice.
Act as if armistice has already arrived.
Celebrate today.

The Poetry of Yoga

Andrea Vincent

RELATIONSHIP

you had no answering machine
so I left a voicemail for you in the sand

could I make the waves wait?

pause

Just long enough

UNION

To Swami Jaya Devi Bhagavati

I rub my palms together, faster, faster,
As if to ignite a campfire from my flesh.
Inhale, pause, exhale, pause.
Inhale, "AUM"
The union of all things.
The sound rumbles from my throat,
the next exhale a higher pitch,
A purer note, filling my skull, my chest an echo chamber,
Ascending my spine like a ladder.
A final note, a lower note,
Descending to my belly, my hips,
To be fully there
An awareness without thought.

The postures flow, a slow and graceful dance.
I morph from one essence to the next:
I am a butterfly,
fluttering my legs as I stretch my groin.
Now I am a cow,
my back sways, my udder grazes the earth.
I arch a cat arch, navel pulled in tight,
Spine raised in hackles.
I salute the sun,
I swan dive into the pure clear water of air.

The Poetry of Yoga

Christina Kaylor

I lunge, I plank.
I am a downward facing dog,
My nose searches the earth for scent,
my tail waggles in happiness.

I slither down, then up, a cobra,
Neck curved back, my tongue hissing in ecstasy.
Feet apart, arms raised in power, I am a peaceful warrior.
I tilt into a star.

Now I am a goddess, thighs laid open,
receptive to the universe.
I stand tall and straight, a mountain;
then, one leg raised,
I become a tree, toes planted in the soil of my mat.
I sway oh so gently in the breeze of the fan,
if only I do not topple over.
So many more selves I am,
I become.

Finally, a corpse:
I lie, limp,
a total relaxation and release of self,
A decomposition, a deconstruction of my what-ness.

The Poetry of Yoga

Christina Kaylor

The circle connects, complete.
My souls rub together, a cricket springing from the earth,
Revived, renewed.

My teacher, now brunette, now blond, now bald,
One person, many people, all the same
A smiling Buddha of pure repose,
A union:
Yoga.

This, I want.
I am.

Repeat:
"Light within me.
Light behind me. Light above me.
Light unto me."

I breathe in the light. I breathe out the light,
Sending it to illumine the darkness.
I re-enter the world, holding my light,
A candle burning within,
Hoping not to extinguish before next week.

LOVE: BLIND AND DEAF

The blind person says to the deaf
Your face is a lovely thing.

    The deaf person says to the blind
    What a sweet song you sing!

The Poetry of Yoga

Laura O'Neale

Looking at a wall of bricks that was "ugly" before
Right after yoga class
I see it shiny as a crystal door
A mirror of my chakras

I go home, light a few candles
While sitting in lotus posture
My eyes are focused on a dot on the wall
My breathing slows down

My crown opens in a thousand petal lotus
Rivers of prana flow through my veins
Thoughts are leaving one by one
Till there is no more worldly nonsense

Only peace and bliss, "It is done!"
Now I understand my responsibility
So I am not talking, nor listening
I just am—infinity

My aura expands
I see it in the "mirror" of the wall
I feel my guru's spirit joining mine
in harmony

You and I unite in a strong bond
I'm holding a huge bowl of light in my hand
Healing light that I offer to all of us
Now we are all one.

EVERYTHING IS A MIRROR

BLESSING WOUNDED CHAMBERS OF THE HEART

Bless the wounded chambers of the heart,
those spaces blackened by loss,
neglect and poisonous thoughts.
Like a field of buried land mines, we step around
these parts, eyes averted, pretending they are not ours.

Turn your gaze towards these dark places
for light cannot show us everything
and sometimes we must sit in the dark
and develop our night vision.

Find an ancient tree with roots that go deep,
sit down and lean against its trunk
as shade drops around you like a beekeeper's net.
The dark is not as empty as you thought.

Night birds call to the lonely spaces in your heart,
cicadas keen, sharing your now-felt grief,
nocturnal animals snuffle at your feet,
and all around you, fungi grow night time vegetation
that cannot survive the pummelling light of the sun.

Stay here a while, quiet, patient, honest, hopeful,
while you wait for a spore to blow in on the wind,
to settle beside you in this shady place.
You will watch it bloom, quicker than expected
in colors not even invented yet.

THURSDAY

Linda O. enters the yoga studio
to tell me she
will not be in class her

best friend
jumped

off a balcony

under the influence of
insomnia medication.

It snows for two days;
pauses
snows again.

Then again for two days.

Three feet and a frosting.
Then more snow.

Shovels stolen from front stoops,
snow up to thighs,
past thighs.

No school for a week,
houses dark, phones down,

10,000 people without heat,
trees in parks,
cracking, cracking.

The world is a blanket,
is clear,
magnificent.

There is no newspaper
delivered this snowy day
with the story of
a woman and a balcony.

A happy woman
on the wrong prescription.

No newspaper report saying
her watchful husband had gone
to the bathroom
for a few seconds.

There were cautions
in the smallest print
we'd find later.
It hadn't yet begun to snow.

If maybe it had.
If maybe she'd been dazzled.

The Poetry of Yoga

Diana Tokaji

Today my husband, being kind and sensitive to the fact that I was
home with the flu offered me some lunch.

He held up the bag from which he'd just pulled two chicken
sausages, the bag cloudy with mucousy juice,
pale links in his hand, dripping.

I am a vegetarian so I refused his offer of a sausage sandwich.
"Not quite what I had in mind," I said.

"What would you like?"

BUTTERNUT SQUASH SOUP

"I was thinking of something along the lines of butternut squash
simmered in spring water with sweet potatoes, carrots, granny smith
apples, onions, zucchini, garlic, fresh ginger, herbs, an
orange, and dashes of cayenne pepper to burn my throat

"blended till creamy and served piping hot with toasted
whole wheat baguette, feta cheese and Greek heather honey."

"Oh," he said.

I love him and I'm learning to bend more so I said,
"If you don't have Greek heather honey,
a ripe avocado will do."

REPEAT OFTEN

during the night
place four stones
on your path for
the next day's journey

when the sun rises
retrieve them
one by one

for they reflect
your dreams of
kindness, honesty
respect and love

then share each
dream with those
you meet that day

The Poetry of Yoga

Shannon Paige

AND HE FELL

Barefoot toting an arm load of newly folded tee blankets,
looking out a studio back window through the rain.
Stumbling, with a cigarette pinned between his fingers,
a little, old, intoxicated man had my attention.
He drew a breath, an extended ash
as he dizzily navigated the sidewalk.
Each step an effort of amazing concentration.

He stepped... stepped. And he fell. From the wet sidewalk,
off the curb, into the street, and straight into a lane of traffic.
His cigarette remained held fast, suspended above earth,
a chin broke his fall and radiated red across the street top.
In an immediate pool of blood,
he crumbled, defeated on the ground like cloth.

Follow me! I burst a battle cry to a fellow staff member.
She leapt from behind the desk,
we gathered the thin man off the street.
We pulled him up to sit on the bus stop bench.
He drew a deep breath from the cigarette he so carefully
protected. "What happened?" He spoke evenly
and gently as blood poured from his chin
down his neck and shirt. "You fell from the sidewalk."
I guarded the panic from my voice turning to a staff member,
"Please, call 911 and bring me a towel and blanket."

In seeming seconds, the blanket and towel arrived.
I bundled him in a little red yoga blanket
held the towel to his chin while waiting for the ambulance

together in the pouring rain.
A protective motherly force rose within me.
He shook with cold and shock. So much blood,
it began to soak through the towel and onto my sleeve.
A small crowd gathered—gazing into our bizarre scene.
"What did she do to him?" One passer by asked another.

The paramedics arrived with an entourage of two squad cars
and a fire truck. The medics expertly gathered him up
one of them turned to me with the studio blanket in his hands,
and said, "This must be yours."

"No, it's his." I responded, "I mean, it's a gift and he needs it.
He should keep it. He is so cold."
The paramedics continued their work.
The original pool of blood was fading and swirling
its final memories into the rainwater
rushing through the gutter towards the drain.

Upon seeing the bright blinking lights pull away from the curb,
I turned on my heels, stepped inside my yoga center,
and padded across the floor to the bathroom.
In the mirror, I saw myself, blood soaked and stained.
The adrenaline gave way to tears,
I slid down the wall—sobbing on the cool tile floor.

"What did she do to him?" The inquiry repeated itself to me.
The tears came harder
I'll tell you what I did to him: I judged him.

The Poetry of Yoga

Shannon Paige

I watched him stagger through rain with distant amusement of
"a little early isn't it pal?" from the warmth of
my establishment.

I'll tell you what I did to him: I cared for him.
From judgment, I was shocked from my comfort zone
and straight to his shaking little side.
When he fell into the street, he fell into my heart
and I fell into immediate service to this stranger.

I'll tell you what did to him: I lied to him to make him feel safe
and held. I held him and lied... until the paramedics pulled up
gathered him into their van with practiced, gloved hands.

I'll tell you what I did to him: I remembered him.
I remembered him as I remembered parts of myself.
I remembered all of my frail aspects and how I, and many that I
love, have been just steps from an emotional gutter more times
than I actually care to remember. I remembered all of the times I
figuratively lifted my negative patterns above the soggy earth
in order to protect them and break a fall or two with my face.

The entire event took less than twenty minutes.
Several days later, I walked into my office
found the little red studio blanket neatly folded on my desk.
"Oh yeah," my husband turned to me, "He brought it back just
a little bit ago. He wanted to tell 'the sweet little girl' who was so
nice to him, 'Thank you.'"

I lifted the little red studio blanket to my chest.
It smelled of cigarettes, rain, and gratitude.
"Thank you, little old man."

I KNOW YOU ARE THERE

I know you are there
I feel you in the longing of my heart
To merge, to become the melody of your song
I see you in the moonlit shimmer on the river,
And the eyes that look back at mine with wild abandon
I hear you as you pluck the strings of my life
and whisper truths in my ears
I taste you in the nectar of sun ripened fruit
and fresh honey comb
I smell you in the fragrance of earth touched by rain,
And the intoxicating scent of Lilies
lavishly revealing their depths
I sense your presence as the carrier of joy and sorrow
The unbiased ever-loving grace of life
The alarm that sounds when I fall unconscious
As the wind that gently tugs at my sleeve
urging me to wake.

The Poetry of Yoga
Vinita Agrawal

MORTAKKA

Sign boards help you get there
by bus or by car and then by boat
the river is the final destination
a womb for the ashes

Mortakka ghat
on the banks of the Narmada
that's where I left you for the last time
Mummy
or was it you who left me forever

Daddy carried you in an earthen pot
all five kilograms of ashes
and some dearly loved bones
that refused to burn
I knew you didn't want to leave

July was wetter than wet
drenched like my heart

Through the rain and the tears
I watched the boat bob madly
on the river of anguish
Daddy balanced himself on its helm

The Poetry
of Yoga

Vinita Agrawal

Slowly the urn
raised shoulder high
released you

I watched my happy times swirl
out of existence

Back on the ghat
something nudged my feet
a little rivulet of water rounding off a stone
like a last caress from you, mummy
I picked it up and kissed it
a tangible treasure
from the ghats that circled life and death.

The Poetry of Yoga

Alexandra Folz

I AM THE SPACE BETWEEN THE BONES

I am the space between the bones,
the synergy that manifests between two points.
I am the expansion depending on my ability to let go.
I am potential that waits for awareness to set me free.

In this place I am infinite.
Yet my potential may not be my reality.
Where is my attention?

If I settle into this bone or that,
I've left the land of expansion.
If I accept this matter of "fact,"
I cease to acknowledge the other point of reference,
the other bone that allows structure to take form.

So I let myself fall over onto that side.
I dive into the other opaque density
that connects and defines form.
Then I go back and forth.

With passionate hip shakes and serpent arms,
I dance this relationship.
And this flutter from one point to the other
reminds me of the illusion of form.

Because
I'm not this bone or that one
I am the pulsing sense that emanates between the two.

WHEN JEWELS SING

Radiance results from earth's pressure,
life working on us with each moments precision
into clear cut uniqueness.

A community of precious human beings
with origins primitive and wild as diamonds,
faceted by skilled and invisible hands that turn us
upon a wheel dusted with God's bright dark silence,
we become men and women joined to walk
swarthy, holy, original and transparent.

Catching first light of day upon ourselves,
our voices sing of truth and loveliness,
in response to vows first sung to us by stars.

The Poetry of Yoga

John Fox

ELBOWS

The sacred quality
of arms, particularly
elbows that make
each of us working class,
put us here for a purpose.
Look at elbows
and what they say:
elbow your way
into the passive crowd
to do what is needed,
give it your elbow grease
this is enough.
Elbows, no one can
possess them because
they can disappear and
you move them
into action by choice.
And that choice
is prayer in action.
The deepest current of love
is not found in the heart.
That is the certain spring,
the natural ease, the flow
from the mountaintop.
The greatest current of love
rushes forward in the choice
to make a cradle of the body.

CONSIDER WHAT HAPPENS

Consider what happens
upon hearing a poem
that moves you. The nod
of your head, tucking
your chin close
to your chest, as if
stopping to rest, as if you could cry now
in the middle of a long journey.
Here, whatever you regret having forgotten
even with your aching tiredness
(which you cannot forget) all of a sudden
turns to a surprisingly vibrant sky
as your eyes widen ever-so-slightly
in a recognition that shimmers
under your skin, wells-up
into a calm line-of-sight
that is your own and goes on
almost forever.
Astonished, you walk outside breathing
and slowly stroll in the fresh air
suddenly aware that back in your house
someone new, a stranger you like,
has arrived.

Dr. Michael Fratkin

STRAWS

If I come to you,
Grasping at straws,
Don't give me a straw.
Lend me your hand.
Give me your time.
Lend me your attention.
Give me your understanding.
Show me the way to the beauty,
Of these sad circumstances.

Please.
Spare me your support for my projected fantasy,
Your soothing whitewash,
Your minty mouthwash.
Please.
Spare me your encouragement,
That it's really not so bad.
It's bad. It's so bad,
Because I love life so much,
That I failed to notice it occurring.
It's bad, and you can feel it.
I know because you cloak me in absorbent tissues,
And you pat my back,
From a safe distance.

The Poetry of Yoga

Dr. Michael Fratkin

While you armor yourself in steel,
While you plug, patch, and plunder,
The wreckage of my emptying heap.
It is a sad miracle,
And a happy one,
And a dazzling one,
And a terrifying one.
It has always and forever been a miracle.
From the amniotic explosion,
To the crackling and crumbling,
Of dust falling gently from the last remaining
Splinters of bone,
Cooling slowly on the bare cinder brick inferno.
From the perfect arc of a three-point shot,
To the broken heart of a foolish teen.
From the ecstatic thrill of an exploring hand,
Under bedsheets, behind a door,
In the fragile solitude of dark sensation.
To the smelling of sex and flowers,
And even, rotting flesh.
From the drone of monotonous complaining,
To working, frustrating.
To indignation, and to righteousness.
It's a miracle. It is.
From top to bottom,
From the beginning to beginning,
To the end.
When I grasp at straws,
Please.
Don't give me one.

The Poetry
of Yoga

Jamie Allison

THE HEART OF GRATITUDE

OM, the Eternal One
Sweet Spirit
Ocean of Possibilities
Beginning-less
Endless River of Creative Power
Divine Mother
Womb of the Universe.

Paint my life with your sacred paintbrush.
Saturate me with the full spectrum of color
so that I may taste every aspect of you that is me.

Let inspiration flow through me
like the illuminative dawn spreading out across the sky
kissing all creation with your spark of love.

Golden Sunlight reflects off your infinite forms
of manifestation creating a mirror for your magnificence.

The Poetry of Yoga

Jamie Allison

Eternity is offering herself as a secret waiting to be told,

a mystery waiting to unfold.

May I imbibe this wonder and drink
from this everlasting cup!

Evening bird song punctuates the quiet hush of twilight.
My heart longs to linger a little longer in

the sweetness of this departing day.

Hold me in the deep blue velvet of your starry night sky.
Bless me with peaceful sleep so that I may welcome a new
day and offer myself fully,
without hesitation to the wonder of this life.

The Poetry of Yoga

Jamie Allison

A TOAST FROM THE UNIVERSE

Look at me, listen to me, spring demands in the voice of a thousand bird songs, in the melting of the frozen creek, with the first shoots of grass pushing their way up through the murky half frozen earth.

Sometimes spring arrives with a terrific wind that shakes the foundation we cling to. Sometimes she arrives quietly, with dark clouds and threatens more winter. She arrives to remind us that even when things look dark, even when the cold chill of winter is hanging on, spring will arrive. Insistent, demanding, look-at-me spring never abandons us.

I'm still here. I never go away she whispers to those who know how to listen. I simply paused and allowed myself to rest, all the while deepening my connection to the earth, staking my claim on future growth. I am always here in the rise and fall of each breath, the dawning of a new day, in each new thought and inspiration. I am the impetus for all that follows. I am the ancient ground from which all arises. I am at once old and new, eternal and ephemeral.

Can we take a chance and be more like spring? Do we have the guts to make ourselves heard? Can we demand to be witnessed? Why is it that we shrink? Why do we turn away from our ancient roots, our right to be here and be heard?

The Poetry
of Yoga

Jamie Allison

Can we dig down deep inside and reconnect to something
bigger? We are rooted in Eternity and yet, we forget.
But we must remember, we must remember,
we must remember.

If we forget for just a moment so much is lost, never to be
retrieved. Each one of us is an expression of love. You were
born to shine your light and to share your love. Don't throw
away the spark of your creative spirit. Don't turn away from
that sacred duty.

Open your heart to the eternal spring of your being.
Expand the boundaries of your love to encompass all
creation. Make your light so bright that you cannot be
ignored. Make your voice so clear that you inspire another.
Make your love so strong that you are never afraid.
Never refuse the fullness of your own heart.

If each one of us demands to be heard, demands to be
seen, demands to love and be loved, the entire fabric of the
universe will celebrate by raising a glass of celestial nectar
to toast your sacred heart and all your auspicious efforts.

MY SACRIFICIAL GROUND

Except you there is nothing
Except you I don't want any thing
The secret of life is in your dancing feet
Thou destroyer of death, O' nectarine light,
Dweller of the burning ground in my heart
All sounds and thoughts I have sacrificed
Aversions and attachments destroyed
Anger and passions reduced to ashes
My ego lies there as a corpse of silence
In the flames of eternal consciousness!
Except you none can stay there!
Except you none can dance there!
Art thou not the light of existence absolute
Dancing in the burning ground of my heart
As blazing truth that exists everywhere
In the splendorous flames of the sun
In the wondrous beauty of the moon
In the stars and lights of the skies
Even in the black holes of cosmic vast
Which bring death to the stars of night
Thou exist in the billions of galaxies
Blazing as brilliant sapphire of consciousness
O' mother Kalika! O' thou, supreme light!
Art thou not the existence absolute, infinite
Dancing in the flames of consciousness
In the sacrificial burning ground of my heart!

DREAMTIME

gypsy dance under a silvery moon
feet sweep out a map in the dirt
distant stars twinkle the way

thru the beat

blackness holds the answers
as much as warm flames
licking air
breathe

golden fields rolling elsewhere
wheat of plenty
of sweet stalk
drifting in violet sky

dreams can be pulled from the soil

damp with earth smell
and the color of memory

INDIA

When I delve, I deliver:
my travel trails
Its been a festival for the road warrior in full flavor
this search

Breathwork with elephants,
horned buffalo and hand cranked sugar cane.

The mantra-quest for a meditative state:
36 hour train rides
tropical blood bacteria,
bearded Baba chai wallahs,
singing Swamis robed glory,
and road-side altars
draped gracefully in banyan trees.

Its brass-bangled chaos
so much on the senses
that my loaded eyes have spent all
their extra energy
on absorbing their surroundings

leaving my nimble fingers at a loss
for the written word.

with no proper *font* for my thoughts.

I scramble to try and scribe
just a sliver of these tales
to carry
their tact
back to you.

But this poem has no translation.
only feet can read these soils.
earthbound beast-horns
braille-bellied and visceral
exhale
evergreen.
raw silk sap

and carry me home to you.

The Poetry of Yoga

Devreaux Baker

RIVER

This river knows nothing but her name
She is the hard blue muscle
that pumps blood into the mouth of morning,
the woman who sits at the edge of sorrow
grafting time into the shape of a clay pot
or reed basket, insatiable with longing
and filled with the ovaries of stars,
the mind of all things drawn to silt and sludge,
to pools and ferns

Currents streak her back with a name
that means dreaming fish, where ripples
of reed ducks and water rats pattern hieroglyphs
against her wide green thighs.
She is the water that we shed as tears,
scooped up by the hands of night
and poured into the throat of day,
turquoise and lapis, emerald and jade.

The moon hums against her skin.
She spirals through a thousand lifetimes
and dances Kali or Quan Yin.
Look, the animals are searching
for their reflection in her face.

Even the God who sleeps
curled in the belly of small creatures
wakes up, slips on her mask of moonlight
and swims from this opening into Mother Ocean.

She splashes their bodies with moss
and now they are snarled
in her net of fish scales and seal bone.
These are the knees of devotion,
the tangled roots of our lives coming to fruition.
The river is a mirror for our bodies.
She carries the planets inside her belly
and hums the earth into being so our bodies,
blooming with their fisted flowers of blood
are filled with that song.

The River, who speaks in tongues, is born and dies
in the fissured cracks of our cells
so that we become the sleeping center of the shell,
the speck of sand turning into pearl.

The Poetry
of Yoga

Devreaux Baker

MORNING POSE

Bare your feet
Repeat the mantra
Of forgiveness
Ask yourself
What does history taste like
Open your heart to sorrow
Open your body to welcome all the directions
Bless the tears your ancestors wept
Learn about survival
Say a prayer for the laying on of hands
Remember the earth beneath your feet
Embrace the lost tribes
Dream of ancient migrations
Be a way-station
For lost souls.

Devreaux Baker

THE NEST

Some people believe trees are lungs, rocks are bones,
rivers are veins.

I kick away from the bank, swim into the
middle of my life.

Light sends spools of silver unraveling
across the surface.

Everything splinters into pieces, nothing remains rooted.
Our neighbor is cutting down one hundred year old trees,
just so their leaves won't fall on his house.

Change wants to work her mantra into each being's heart.
I let the water hold me.
This is when the part from last night's dream
surfaces inside me.

A bird flew to me carrying her baby in her mouth.
She settled it in my lap and flew away to look for food.

She kept coming back to sit in the bowl
of my calves and thighs,
feeding her baby from out of the nest
my body had become.

Alanna Kaivalya

THE ARMS OF GRACE

And so often, I pray for grace,
if only from that shallow place
where my mind meets my body
and I'm looking for answers
to questions unformed
in that sea of storms
that can be found in the heart
It doesn't always come easy
but when it comes,
it comes naturally
when I let myself be held in that perfect surrender
the mind goes and the heart stops
and there is only god
only the love that comes
when you know you're held
in the arms of the beloved
hope dawns with that tiny spark
of the small flames within the heart
of the darkness of the soul
that cannot be measured
where we have to feel along with our hands
and our trust, and where missing a step
would turn us to dust
only to rise again like a phoenix from the ashes
the cycle is constant and unbroken
despite our wavering
despite our arguing
and despite our misunderstanding
we can never know what we already know
far beyond our mind and somewhere within our soul
that happens only at the end of the edge
where there is nowhere else to fall
but into the arms of grace

The Poetry of Yoga

Margaux Delotte-
Bennett

A MOVEMENT PRAYER

arms stretched up and out
heart
mind
eyes
soul
all open wide
lunging towards peace

CROSSROADS

standing at the crossroads of dying in fear or living bravely
eyes open to the possibility that this might be it
this might just be the last poem I write

did I laugh enough?
love enough?
learn enough to boldly let go of this shell?
I knew this day would come
so grateful it's not by gun, disease or angry hands
but possibly by water and sand
what is there yet to understand?

this might be the last poem I write
did I paint enough pictures with my words?
envision a new world through my songs?
did my soul bear witness to my voice?
my art to my soul?
my pen to my art?

The Poetry of Yoga

Margaux Delotte-
Bennett

this might just be the last poem I write
I will go laughing into the grave
because my mind has never known such peace
through my travels I have been made whole
my flesh, my sex, my hair and breath,
tongue and soul all one
eyes open because I need to see this
I made it to this moment
when my last poem
might just be

Om Sat Chit Ananda Para Brahma
Purushothama Param Athma
Shri Bhagavathi Sametha
Shri Bhagavathe Namaha

The Poetry of Yoga

Kitty Arambulo

KAIVALYA

Palms together in gratitude
to ancient lines of wisdom
a tribute

Life's challenges met through practice
worldly worries fade away
on the mat

Body, mind and breath in unison.
Devotion leads to light
with grace

Glimpsing stillness, moments of wholeness
with attention, focus
and surrender
pure joy.

Freedom.

THE RAY

the time is running
slowly
the hearts are beating
furiously
the shadows dance
wildly
the darkness rules
all over

cry sparks
a ray is born
a ray of light
and blessing

CHANGE THE CHANNEL

In this hit-movie called Life, Drama is full.
Watching the negatives bust out of my genes.
Critical inner guidance turns into rage.
Spiral of prana leaking out.
It's time to change the channel.

CLICK!

Turn the DVD player off.
Naturally, "creation" button turns on.
Write, draw, paint, dance, act, play...
Inner candle is re-lit.
Feed the flame with care and love.
The outer now grows and glows,

In Peace.

SOLSTICE POEM

Black & white wear
each other's clothes
and the darkest moment

is that moment
when the dark
lets go.

The thing to do, I guess,
is love the darkness
knowing darkness

also disappears.
And trust the light
though it

comes & goes
and makes no promises.

The Poetry of Yoga

Joan Dobbie

YOGA CLASS THE TEACHER SPEAKS

We sit straight
Hold our hands open as cups
Breathe deep swelling breaths
My lips form familiar words
But I am not speaking
It is the mother who is speaking
Out through the channel
Of my throat
I am riding on the dark resonance
Of her voice
That is not my voice
But hers
I listen as she speaks
She is telling us now
To come touch each other
I feel other hands move warm into mine
I glance at the clock
We have one human hour
The room is darkening
The mother is saying to close our eyes
We do
And we see vast distances inside of ourselves
We see infinite darkness & there we find color
We are watching our blood flow
In rich salty rivers
We are touching the ivory metal of bones
Our bodies are flowing in rhythm

With the centuries
Slow as a tide moving over an island
We are mist bringing life to dark clay

Making flesh
Moving our flesh over ivory bones
I listen with heart expanding
I listen with mind carefully tuned
I speak but the voice is not mine
All ears are turned inward
The mother is speaking
Of peace
Her voice that is sweet like the worlds
That are breathing within us
Is speaking of peace
Is speaking of peace
We are joined in the flow of the breath
Of her breathing
The mother is flowering
The mother is flowering
I listen I hear words
I listen I hear words & winds
I listen I hear winds & waters
We are swimming in the dark honey
Of the song of our mother
We are holding together like the cells
That make up a creature
We are breathing one breath like the breath
Of the planet
Not sleeping nor waking
And still we are watching
With visions that rise to a place
Some call heaven
We are joined in a blessing
That is ours for the asking
We are vessels of peace
We are vessels of peace

VARANASI

Oldest inhabited city of the world,
Streets swarm with the dust of ancient memories
Held by the elders... the life/salvation cycle.

People travel from far and near to your shadow shores.
Pilgrims of possibility seeking moksha,
relief from mortal seasons of struggle.

First seen at dusk, as the day ends and evening begins,
as the sun sets and the moon rises,
full in her magical, mystical splendor.

Cremation fires mark the shoreline,
blazing intense heat while lighting the dark sky,
even as Ganga G. flows cool and steadily onward.

Grievers mourn, dones stoke the fires,
bodies bathed in the river's holy water,
then left on the shore to dry,
as those who witness silent and still,
viewing the unimaginable, sacred ritual.

Ancient Vedic chants, chakra bells,
powerful percussions pervade the senses,
as priests prepare the nightly Arati Ritual
celebrating the river Ganges yet another day
and signaling its close for the night.

Full moon illuminates the long wooden boats
marking their silent return from fiery death to steeping ghats,
creating our own ritual along the way.

The Poetry of Yoga

Dr. Seena Russell Axel

Our prayers for the departed ones left floating
on the river of individual sorrow.

Ancient wooden vessels dot the shoreline,
as Brahim priests begin the Arati.
Smoke from their fire dance create a bridge between worlds,
as all who witness the sacred ceremony sit
and float... like lotus
in silent awe.

All is still. All is ancient.
We sit together as one.
We've done this before throughout the ages,
even as we sense again, as if for the first time.

The cycles of life and death provide a silken thread,
connecting us to all.

Here... there is nothing.
Here... there is everything.

And our hearts silently chant... OM!

Shelly Bhoil Sood

DUST

Name is the 'Number'
of soul's imprisonment
in body

Face is the 'Keep'
of desire's trust
in body

Fame is the 'Echo'
of the empty vessel, the body

What is
is the dust
that alone lived
the nebula
and will alone live
the earth.

BUT BALANCE

Expiry is
in the making of wooden bodies
with granite heads
packed in the match-box coffin

combustible on either side

to rub against life
might tatter and scatter bodies
igniting dry cracked flesh

to live contained
may moist the granite

and save the wood
to burn its funeral.

The Poetry of Yoga

Ainne Frances
dela Cruz

In my old age
My parents have decided
To give me space:
A room of my own
Complete with a bed
And a view of the
Woods beside our house.

As the body grows older
It grows inflexible, it seems.
Either that
Or my bed is too hard
I can't sleep nights.

My muscles involuntarily
Curve to an imaginary space
You occupied
Lifetimes ago.

TRANSIENT

I feel the strain of living
Whenever my cheek touches
Bedsheets, made rough-smooth
By the spin-dry cycle of
The washing machine
Downstairs
I open my windows
To the elements.
I laugh at the face
Of cyclones.

There is no reason
To stay.
Why will I
Miss this place?

BUDDHA BEADS

Green-black-red-yellow
Beads of light, escape
From my hand, stuck
On a forest of hair.
Buddha beads are supposed
To protect, its circle
Encircling the wearer
Devotee, a prayer wheel
To nirvana.

I am no believer, yet
Strung there, my arm
Feels like a million
Strobes of light courting
Blue-black skin gleaming
Stuck to my bones.

My hand becomes
A pathway to the dark,
Envelopes of secrets
Lost to the touch, beads
Of light spring up
Like St. Elmo's fire
Beckoning, beckoning.

THE SOUND OF SERVICE

Service speaks
softly
quietly
carefully

Unknown hands
deliver great deeds
with little or no greed

The sound of service
seeks not to claim
name
fame
or even shame

True service
rises above
good
bad
happy
sad

It can be said
that in service

with divinity

there is no success

For the process is, was
and will be
endless

And therein lies
its greatness

A heart of service

can never fail
For to truly serve another
is to become
like a mother:
selfless
content
and strong

Giving fully
and completely

The secret of service's
nobility
lies in its connection

The hands that serve
are full
even as they become
empty
For to serve
is to love
To love is to give
To give with love
is to forgive
the faults in others

To clear the eyes
so that we may truly
and deeply
see
All that we may
Be
When we become
as One
and are
Free

The Poetry of Yoga

Panda

BE NOW

Stop carrying the past and future
Lighten the load
It must be tiring, to hold and hold
All our concepts, so very old
Can't you see, we can't be free
As long as we carry that certain 'me'
Just leave the past and future too
Just react to what is now
From stillness we will find
Motivation to move in time
Without effort we feel so free
So leave your thoughts and be free
Then you'll know it's absurd
The past and future never occurred!

MASKED BALL

Drop all our clothes, or names and ideas
'Become naked'
become who we really are
when the falseness falls away
What's left?
What stays?
It's just a smile a laugh or tear
In no mind, where is the fear?
Be naked
Drop the clothes
Spirit arise
The light of our beings
Without the disguise

The Poetry of Yoga

Ellen Crow Vodicka

THE ASSIGNMENT IS TO SIT

to sit
what an adventure!
to sit with nothing and with everything
with difficulty and surrender
with humility and wonder
I sit and search for that luminous river that enlivens
my spine
searching with my body, unbridled by mind
channeling an amoebic ancestor as the breath
undulates belly to breast
I feel like an infant learning to hold myself upright
I feel like an old woman as my shoulders ache and
cave in
a rusted padlock wedged between my shoulder
blades fights to stay locked
the breath moves with fluid fingers, to pry me open
again
the earth receives me in her familiar nest of gravity
my chest fills with birds
ribs spread wide and cirrus
throat lengthens hollow stem
palms weighted with their own warmth

The Poetry of Yoga

Ellen Crow Vodicka

fingers awkward, curled, childish
slow stirring hips
jaw slack at last
eyes cradles in their sockets
just sit, just sit
a thought floats up and bursts into a
hundred more seeds of thought
breath changes with the textures of memory
a belief lands like a brick or rises like a sun dog

I am classroom, teacher, student, the chair,
the blank page, the furious

pencil my back aches, my mind yawns
the dog is more friendly to me, the cat sits on my lap
the house is freezing, the sky outside is a concrete gray
the wind shakes the walls
I fumble along with love
I feel ancient, timeless, the first rumor of an ocean,
the first chance at consciousness
I sit, I sink, I float
just this
a moment
a slice of time as tender and translucent as an eyelid
a second, a full second
of poetry

The Poetry of Yoga

Ellen Crow Vodicka

EMBODIMENT

When I begin
to re-inhabit my native land
I can feel how my self-consciousness has sinuously slipped in
there are jammed doors in my shoulders
my spine secretes secrets and keeps mum,
my hips won't give their honey
everything is conch quiet with an ocean roaring within
there is a prayer uttered in a lost language written under the skin
when i begin
to detach from the word and feel the power
of limb singing to limb
unwinding the long scroll of torso
feet finding the invisible path
sweat chasing maps to erase them
and I begin again
breasts sway and slap
palms birth suns

The Poetry of Yoga

Ellen Crow Vodicka

womb

beat

one

I become the ancient circle of ancestors keeping time in unison

the village clapping and trilling, wrapped around the fire of my belonging

the midwife waiting in the corner rocking

the mother moaning with her body unfolding

dancing all night through the dark tunnel and pulse of stars

dancing until the sticky skin dries and falls like a skeletal leaf

softly shattering in the wind

dancing until the bridge collapses the current is unleashed

until I forget how to swim

and am swallowed in one gulp

crowning in an ecstatic release

sliding into the air

crying open

my glistening new born native

body

The Poetry of Yoga

Ellen Crow Vodicka

UP FROM THE UNDERWORLD

Knowing something
about the fullness of the world's sadness
and the fullness of the world's joy,
I don't know how to proceed.
It's not easy, this walk through fire, still
I run, torched and sputtering, to leave
a small heap, an offering.

I could lie down on the dying grass,
with a smile full of pomegranate teeth.
Laughing, let my mouth spill garnet seeds.
I could be spring's wet rupture under a blossom moon.

I want the momentum of birth after a thousand deaths,
I want to do what I'm scared to do,
to do what I love, to follow
the embroidery of blood mapping my ancestors' voice
to where I have not been yet.

The key to resurrection is to re-member.
Remember pain shooting through you wet and tender,
Agonized in your growing, the heart
Sharply green in its need.
You never know who will split your darkest seeds,
to draw light from your eyes.
Remember, we are golden with benevolence.
Like spare change angels, we all pocket some redemption.
Give in
to one
thirsty kiss

Kneel at your heart
and drink.

THE HILL

The place where time is left behind
Where souls dance free-spirited
Oneness
Stillness
Nothingness
But Everything is here
An escape to solitude
To where we came from
To find the Self and listen to it
Freedom
Truth
Discovery
The interconnectedness of life
Like the missing piece of a puzzle
The 'aha!' moment
When teardrops fill your eyes
As the self sees the Self for the first time
The pulse of the Universe flowing through my veins
It's all the same
So this is what it feels like?
I breathe in the view
It's a long way down
So I store this moment in my mind
Knowing what must be done
And begin my descent
Back to where I started

MY PRACTICE

I am calm and steady
rooted in my truth
I am graceful and flowing
guided by the winds of my breath
I am strong and powerful
unshaken by the chaos of my wounds
But I am forever reminded
by the vulnerable nature of my soul
When I see the fire, I embrace the cosmic ritual,
and I ask Kali to purify my sins
Nothing can remove my connection to the source
For I hear my calling,
and I answer the nadas of the divine
This is my moment to inhale
the beauty of love, faith and truth
My passionate spiritual flow pours honey into my life

AWAKEN

Open your eyes and awaken to the beauty of a new day
The world is waiting for the sun
The the rays of your heart
Waiting for you to dance in the true nature of your veins
Rejoice in the pulsate from your you
Awaken that and step into you
Sing loudly to the rhythms that awaken

The Poetry of Yoga

Jeffrey Cohen

TAHINI AND THE BEE

I made a lunch of lentils, quinoa, collards & sauerkraut
covered in kimchi and tahini.
The bee came curious, looking for something to make honey.
I winced a little in fear of being stung,
but mostly allowed him to be.
Daring a closer look, a piece of quinoa got stuck to his wing,
and a drop of tahini near that place where he stings.

Immediately, I noticed the change of his focus,
he was grounded and could not fly.
Crawling around the edge of the plate, he worked toward
an escape, by incessantly flapping his wings & hind legs
which scraped the place near his stinger.
Soon the grain of quinoa flew off with little effort.
I was relieved, but not the bee,
the tahini gave too much to gravity.
The wings gave a hum, but nothin' done,
he was stuck like pulling a knife from your back.

What shall I do?
I see the tan goo. Could I wipe it away and induce liberation?
Could he be still long enough so I could get just a touch
without triggering his instinct for protection?
If I help, and he stings, he dies.
If I do nothing and he can't fly, then he dies.
As if to ask him what shall I do, I studied his moves,
and realized he was giving me a lesson on listening.

"There may be a time when I let you take away my burden, so
stay with me. I might make it through by effort and pursuit,
but you won't know unless you stay with me."

So I placed my napkin close and he crawled on the cloth
carpet, sensing the absorbent sheet. Turning to my lunch, I
gazed on his struggle to release the tahini from his hind part.

For quite awhile the battle waged on, with no indication
of progress. In fact, it was distress.
He fought valiantly, for a place he could not reach or see.
What I had not noticed was the microscopic progress
from each stroke of his leg,
releasing a molecule of ground sesame.
What to him was process was a flick of the switch to me,
and all of a sudden he was close to being free.

Just a pin needle's worth left. Then it was gone!
And then the bee... sat there.
As if to exhale and say, "Ok, let's see."

He lifted an inch in flight, the first since the start of his plight.
I wondered, 'has a bee ever gone 30 minutes
without suspending his body?'
True nature revived, he took to the sky, with ease,
Actually
Quite
Nonchalantly.

His freedom was unexpected joy to me.
To witness the struggle, not taking it away, not risking the
sting, but all the while remaining loving.
I couldn't do it for him,
But in allowing the bee's being
I gave no reason for the stinging.
No reason for my suffering, no reason for his dying.
And that sent me flying, too.

The Poetry of Yoga

HawaH

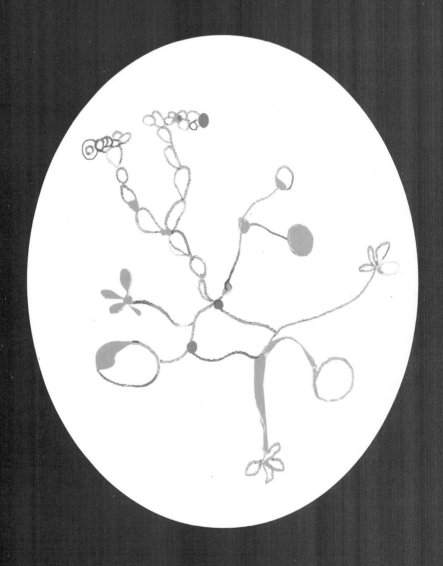

DESTINY

We are the water
before it gains a reflection

A snail
that wished to move faster

A fish
that desired to walk on land

A stone desiring to feel

Yael Flusberg

WHAT I TELL MYSELF WHEN I GO OUT OF MY MIND

When boredom comes to you as a gray boulder,
picture your ankles bound by chains
beside a frost-bitten road. Shackle yourself
to Dennis Brutus, the poet imprisoned alongside
Mandela, on an island made of metamorphic rock
off the coast of the Cape in a thick morning fog,
hammering stone to gravel.

The clouds will piss pellets of leaden ice.
Lug your hunk along in a silver shopping cart
so the walk from stoop to store mimics
monotonous donkey work.

For now, you don't have to do anything.
If symptoms of worldly withdrawal are worrying,
then bless your boulder with your eyes.
Get close, note how striated its body, like aged teeth,
that slate comes in as many shades as restlessness.

A poet I know walks the woods by her house
talking to the dead. Thank You Father Stone
she'll whisper as she sinks her sit-bones
into its cold cradle, a moment of rest.

Yael Flusberg

Sometimes the unbearable ennui is God gearing
you up and off the grid so you can chip away at your
condition as client or consumer, your city crushed into a
market, your neighbors
broken into an unfortunate demographic;
all you love reduced to bundles of metallic bricks
buried in a concrete vault somewhere below the asphalt.

So you get bored when you fail to feel the power of the
plates pushing up collisional boundaries.
You can build mountains
with what's inside.
Plant an ear atop bedrock and hear
the bass in its voice as it vibrates a Mourner's Kaddish,
a heavy-handed metaphor for the gift of weighted time
which pulverizes ambition,
leaving it behind its own dust.
Let the smoky rock roll over your bones
until it finds its bearing.
When the moon is balsamic, cast the weight aside.

It can take a million years to create
even the smallest pebble.
Know that a time will come when
you'll exchange dreaded days
for that fleeting feeling of being unburdened,
able to see
slivers of faceted crystals among the finest ash.

The Poetry of Yoga

Shakti Sunfire

THE SYMPHONY OF SILENCE

Secret, this silence of depth and healing,
where the old stories are woven like
silvery threads,
the web tracing lines of lilting light.

Silence, in sacred serendipity,
you create
the symphony
with your pauses of perfect punctuation.

Without you life would be
a monotonous drone,
like the buzzing of a fluorescent light, noticed only at
the beginning and end.

It is in you Silence,
this pre-cognitive place
of pregnant possibility,

form
grows excited to unveil it's masterpiece.
And it is to your depth that form returns,
full and spent, at sweet, sighing sunset.

Silence.
Not empty but unfathomably full
You whisper secrets to those who know to listen.
You speak of

love,
of trust,
of friendship,
of freedom.

Silence, I have only begun to know you.
You,
and your artful affirmation.
Let me roll out the red carpet of my life for you to walk upon,
and wholeness of me, we agree, will be your throne.

It is that grand, my welcoming.
Secret, this silence of depth and healing,
where the old stories are woven like
silvery threads,
the web tracing lines of lilting light.

Keep making
your music, and I dance
to the world inside this one.
Where love moves
with no agenda
and
we
are not
confused.

Silence.
I hear you.
I am listening...
at last.

UNTITLED

There you are, sitting under the stars
watching and waiting and hoping and praying
that one will shoot across the sky

and when it does you'll make a wish
hoping for true love a sight from high above
hoping is not just for fools

and like the waves, hope will ebb and flow
but the true peace of mind comes from
knowing in time
we're all hoping for the same dream

one day it comes, you find true love
a love that is pure and able to cure
the emptiness inside your heart

this true love, won't ebb and flow
its connection is sound

The Poetry of Yoga

Jason Nemer

upon sacred ground
and blessed by the stars in the sky

what's this love, fallen from above
it's the love of the earth to the creatures she births
unconditional just like the sun

so now that you have found true love,
the sages all know that to love is to grow
closer to god every day

so when you asked for a shooting star
the divine light has sparked

your potential of here
we're all hoping for the same dream
yes we're all hoping for the same dream
we're all hoping for the same dream

A DYNAMIC TRANSFORMATION

It has been too long
since the words told me
how I really feel

These days I speak less
with my pen and brush
more with my body and breath

It is hard to write about
experiencing a dynamic transformation
that sounds so unreal

The grace at which I can now move
in and out of each pose
reflects the pace at which my life now flows

The fear I overcame to stand on my head
becomes a reflection of the fear
I overcame just to live

Now trying to give this
transformation away
to someone else

The question is
how can I teach something
impossible to understand myself?

How can my life be so different
just because I learned to touch my toes?

BALANCE

My breath expands and contracts.
· It is reflexive, restless, disrespectful,
spiritual and utterly calm.
I've tried for weeks
to stand on one leg.
I am showing improvement
but still can't get the knack.
It's just a matter of placing bone on
bone.

This morning
I sat,
a cup of tea in my lap,
looking at my library
and its inordinate disarray of books.
I felt
in awe of my past,
a negligible history
that is all my own
and all I own.

And I fell to my knees
in gratitude and grief
(thinking of the brilliance of Tocqueville,
the compassion of Freud,
Melville's largeness of heart),
and I sought to make amends
for all my disregard.

That night
I carried my wife's
nearly weightless thongs
up the bedroom stairs,
a very small act of love.
A pile of newsprint and magazines
lies on her side of the bed.
On mine, volumes of poetry.
Preparing to retire
I felt inexplicably useful,
filled with the expectation
that I would arrive
at a state of perfect balance,
perched upright, not alone,
but standing firmly...bone on bone.

The Poetry of Yoga

Danielle Margosian

TEN PERFECT BREATHS

inhale, freshness and renewal
noticing traffic jams where the prana's stuck
releasing the stresses of today, letting tensions melt away
exhale, frustration and impatience
banished from the timeless zone
defined by a lilac rectangle of mat
> pause in the emptiness
>> one

inhale, wonder and curiosity
childlike playfulness and excitement to explore
destinations unknown or visited before
exhale, boredom and limitations
recognizing it's only perspective that makes life seem dull
the difference between seeing a glass half empty or half full
making a seemingly impossible goal achievable
> pause in the anticipation
>> two

inhale, courage and inspiration
pushing the limits, redefining what success is
exhale, fear and apathy
knowing falling hurts far less than the regret of never trying
> pause in the confidence
>> three

inhale, connectedness and unity
appreciating fellow yogis
then expanding to feel oneness with all beings
exhale, selfishness and loneliness
the root of many mental afflictions
disabling our high-tech fragmented society
> pause in the collectiveness
>> four

The Poetry of Yoga

Danielle Margosian

inhale, grace and forgiveness
believing all beings are worthy of it, including self
offering this gift whenever we encounter brokenness
exhale, stubbornness and resentments
choosing to let go of bitter thoughts and memories
that interfere with healing energies
   pause in the release
     five

inhale, compassion and service
flowing through asanas with a higher purpose
dedicated to those hurting or in need
praying for burdened bodies and spirits to be freed
exhale, indifference and excuses
seeking to notice the surrounding needs
taking action to give better than receive
   pause in the commitment
     six

inhale, wisdom and truth
embracing the learning process, even when life's
lessons are tough
resisting the temptation to give up
exhale, ignorance and lies
destroying the chorus of voices speaking negativity
roles that play out our insecurities
   pause in the understanding
     seven

inhale, balance and flexibility
adjusting according to circumstance
flexing and extending, creating a vinyasa dance
exhale, confusion and rigidity
not stuck inside the box, but open to new possibilities
   pause in the spontaneity
     eight

The Poetry of Yoga

Danielle Margosian

inhale, hopes and dreams
unspoken desires of a pure and dedicated heart
seeds planted, ideas born, future visions appear
like the rainbow after a storm
exhale, depression and defeat
gathering strength to continue fighting
warriors, raising our hands in victory
        pause in the battle
           nine

inhale, love
feeling it swirling thru the body
all channels open and broadcasting clearly
prana coursing evenly
from trickles in the fingertips
to rushing river past the hips
everything moving freely
mind and body at peace and ease
exhale, love filled to overflowing
and the goodness keeps on growing
savoring each breath's completion as we meditate
        pause in the sacred space the yoga creates
          ten

        ten perfect breaths.

THOUGHTS on LOVE

Some things remind me of you
I don't know why.

See me there with my hands outstretched
Shaped like a bowl.
Cupping within them the glimmer of a rough gem
That is my love offering to you...
With a smile on my lips
And a sureness in my gaze
That belies the question in my heart.

If my fingers—this vessel—held tight together,
suddenly spread apart,
And the love were to pass like sand through them
Would we gather each grain together from the ground,
Or would I kneel down alone?

SUDDENLY

As if a veil were lifted
there's no more distance
between me
and you.

Joanne G. Yoshida

ALWAYS WANTING MORE

I want to spend the night with

you again.

To rest with you.

Just rest.

Like that.

All the rest

of days.

The Poetry of Yoga

Joanne G. Yoshida

SEVENTEEN

(FROM AROUND THE FOOL MOON)

Can you teach me,
Ocean, how do you begin
Each wave
Where is the point that you
Lift up from your
Volumes
And rise one
Billowing sail
Fill it with
Breath and release it
Back into
Yourself

THE HUMAN HEART

When I approached yours,
I was surprised how it
opened up to let me enter.
I walked slowly and
softly, marveling at its vastness.
It was then I knew,
that I was the first person who'd explored
these walls.
Once inside, enveloped by its fresh warmth,
I stopped
and listened.
For what else does one do
inside a heart.

LITTLE ONE

Oh lord please do not let this life be a race
If it is i do not care to win or even place
I've now seen life begin with its first breath
A desperation and a high
The beginning of the test

Thank you little one for introducing me to me
1 + 1 truthfully equals three

There will be days when i make you laugh
Days when i make you cry
Some days you will feel low
Some day you may get high

So thank you little one for choosing me
A true intention has now been born
You have come to me in the most beautiful form

In my hands dear
Your life will know no fear
I will guide you through the delusions and pains
I will provide you shelter from the metaphysical rains
Your cries to me will be a sweet growth
Strengthening for your lungs
new life has begun

Each day will pass like a flicker of light
When it feels too fast i promise to hold you tight
Thank you little one for reminding me
The present moment is where i need to be

Now i lay in bed with your heart to mine
With your mother close to our side
There is nothing left for me to find

Thank you little one for setting me free
For you are all
I ever dreamed

UNTITLED

I flow and love paints me
I lift and love sings me
I ground and love harmonizes me
I align and love sculpts me
I spiral and love dances me
I contract and love teaches me
I expand and love rains me
I engage and love laughs me
I fold and love prays me
I bow and meet your eyes
and love connects me

The Poetry of Yoga

Elizabeth Barnett

FATHOM

there is one thing
it doesn't exist
but everything that exists
exists in it
what we experience is a prodding into
a bending of poking of stretching of
bouncing back of a thing that doesn't exist
how unfathomable
and we fathom it
isn't that beautiful?

BUDDHI

I can't read it
Craft it... or think it into existence
Poetically describe it so I can hide behind the language
Pretend it so it can be my illusionary counsel
So I can appear stronger, older, supreme
to the insecure me

I've wondered how I can perform it
Find the future and record it
Instead I wait patiently for it to ignite within
And when it builds, I let it boil
If it spills, I let the burns tattoo me
Document itself on me, remind me
For the days when I'd like to play ignorant or dumb
Or when I want to be something other than what
I've become

I close eyes to open intuition
Beg for it to come faster than slower
Plead with it so it can be pretty and sweet
Maybe even flatter my form
Make me have that royal laugh and the knowing nod
Or a special place at the family table
Let it give me applaud, or at least give me grace
Let it disguise the uncertainty on my youthful face
Give me substance to tell someone, to save someone
To save myself

I want it, love it, need it for salvation, but resist it
When it comes most authentically
It comes in lessons learned
Experiences earned
Gifted situations give opportunity to take off

Old spectacles and simply see

The Poetry of Yoga

Helina Metaferia

LIGHT FLUSHING

I hear melodies that are silent to others
See orbs of brilliant colors while they all stare blind
Speak in tongues that belong to our cousin planets
Breathe in rainbows and exhale gold dust
Dance spirals in a linear world

Each time I close my eyes I travel years back and years
Forward... until now is thickly painted across my eyelids
More vividly than pupils could ever witness
More perfectly than sight was meant to be
Vision reaches beyond form and becomes consciousness

I listen to silence and find instructions
Where to find art in chaotic yesterday
How to heal wounded guts with laughter
How to engineer monuments in neighboring dimensions
I record the lessons in Spirit and I recall during the tests

I live a life that is rich beyond his dollars or her furs
I live in exuberance, in a light lifting souls on an exodus
Home... in a light that misses most when they beckon for
Home... in a light that exists most when you are stranded all
Alone... calling upon strength from the Creator

Call it sensitivity, a glitch, an awakening
Call it by a name, call it by a definition, call it by a diagnosis
Call it for control purpose
Call it before it calls you and claims you
Or simply let it be

I know
How beautiful it is
To belong to the other side of the mirror

TEACHING UNION

The Bridge is a diaphragm
of muscle

Connecting chest cavity
to abdominal cavity

Under it the Colorado River flows
backward

Dividing Time
from time.

A knife with a second hand
cuts the air in retrograde motion

Breathe out, using the muscles
of the bridge
to exhale completely

You have been on vacation
an awfully long time.

LIVING IN THE WORLD

When hearing the teachings,
I cannot listen.
When meeting the teacher,
I cannot see.
Does memory strike even chords?
Can the intellect become less clever?
And when, as a child, did I learn to mind the distance?
If ego is a pattern,
Can the waves break the form?
Not being of the body,
What are the thoughts?
Not being of the thoughts,
What is the body?
Not knowing the purpose,
The aim is less sharp.
Losing the purpose,
The questions are confusing.
Coming into nothing is knowing more.
The simplest instruction
Is the most difficult to follow.
A difficult instruction may miss the point.
Where silence is mistaken as strength,
No one is heard.
This is the smell of the world.

Ellen Morais

ASANA

I am like clay, Dervish spinning on your wheel
Putty, pliable in your craftsman's hands
Turn after turn, I dance for you
Undulate beneath your careful touch, your expert eyes
Breasts, hips, lips, thighs, breath

You smooth and warm my skin, knead out the knots,
blend the worry from my brow
Like a warm blade on butter, you melt my resolve
and I drink you in
Let you mold me into something of your design
You carve out the beauty I hide within
Make plain, what others do not see

Willing to be your creation, I bend myself into the mold
of your artist's hands
Stretch toward your agile fingers
Wrapping them around me like a coat
And wait with anticipation as you bring me close
Paint the colors of my skin then place me in the light
so that I am revered

When you go I am distraught
Gazing at my reflection with a timid realization
laced in doubt
I am amazed at what I see
Even I didn't know what I could be until now
Dropping disbelief like veils to the floor,
I embrace myself
And I am born.

The Poetry of Yoga
of Yoga
Eileen Olson

OUR TURN

I turned to Yoga for stress and found
Peace.

I turned to Yoga for movement and found
Stillness.

I turned to Yoga for flexibility and found
Stiffness.

I turned to Yoga to escape and found
Love.

I turned to Yoga to find friends and found
Solitude.

I turned to Yoga to find happiness and found
Bliss.

The Poetry of Yoga

Tommy Rosen

SAT NAM

...Was Born On An Inhale

As much time as possible with my family and friends
As many balls as I can run down in the outfield
As many movies, tv shows and books that I can take in
As many epic meals that i can have
As much time on my mat and sitting as I can muster
As many books as I can write
As many lives as I can touch
As much love as I can make
As much time with my wife as I can get
Oh my god,
I'm addicted to everything!
Sat Nam, Sat Nam, Sat Nam
Sat Means Truth
Nam means Identity
Truth is my identity

Died On An Exhale...

THE MONK'S MEANINGLESS ADVICE

Perched high on a cloud-topped mountain,
an old monk drinking Tibetan Chai.
I asked him for the sacred key to life
and this was his diamond-reply.

"First, you have to learn to be alone.
To be bored and still content.
To have no need for friends, lovers, or family,
no need for high status, fame and luxury.

"To love yourself as you really are,
behind the mask you advertise.
To accept the mental reality, the ups and downs.
To accept your deep suffering and ma-rigpa,
without arrogance or pretence.

"Then, you have to learn to love your friends and family;
Unconditionally, without hope of return,
even when they don't need or want you any more.
To value their happiness more than your own.
To understand that when they gave birth to you
they sowed the seed for your death.

"Then, you have to learn to love complete strangers,
Those whose lives hold little interest to you.
The rubbish collector, the shop-keeper,
the waitress and the bus driver.

The tramp, the whore, the banker, the street-sweeper.
All of humanity as Interdependent.
To see their kindness as like that of a mother.
To fully realize they want happiness just like you.
Yet, what they run after, like you, leads to more and more dis-
appointment and dis-ease.

"Then, you have to learn to love your enemies.
Those who harm, hate and envy you.
Who spread lies and malicious gossip about you.
Who belittle and humiliate you.
View them like finding a precious jewel in the mud.
One can never tame the mind without them.
Like a crazy son we should love them,
even more than ourselves.
For they will lead us to patience and compassion,
To the wisdom of emptiness.
Revere them like a great teacher."

At that he smiled and giggled like a child.
As if it were the simplest, yet most difficult thing to do.
"But if you can't manage to do that, don't worry."
He sparkled, "Be like an autumn leaf floating down a river.
Because there is really no-thing to do.
Ultimately, whatever advice I gave you,
is all meaningless too."

Jacquelyn Browne

WHAT THE CAT KNOWS

Outside the quarter moon shines its
Pearled luminescence at me and my cat
Through the window onto our bed
My husband on one side
Me on the other
And our cat in the middle
I reach to feel his warm smooth fur
He looks at me and makes his way through

The crackles of our down comforter
To nestle and purr against my body
I turn and we lie, cat being and human being, spine to spine
Delighting in our bony commonalities
I focus on his purr
Surely his purr is the way to breathe into now.

UNTITLED

There is more than self,
yet all is contained in the Self:
vessel, conduit, instrument of being
in the world as we know it,
in the ways the world can be known.
In it, yet not of it, Sufi teachings say.

You must learn to love
what is incomprehensible,
the mystery beneath every moment,
each leaf or petal that unfolds in its own time,
each wave that rises only to sink back,
every form of being whether or not
it pleases you. Make it your life's work.
Make it your life's work.

SOMETIMES IT'S NOT ENOUGH

I try to be good,
but sometimes it's a thin veneer,
as Freud said, a thin veneer of civilization.
The beast lives in all of us, the return of the repressed.
The beast stares through our eyes,
dark, cold, glittering eyes in civilized faces.

I know why "they" kill,
and rob,
and rape.
"Nothing human is alien to me."
I know why young men make war,
why war is a natural state,
why the Golden Rule is an ideal.

It's true.
I meditate all day long.
That's what it takes to repress the beast.
I meditate as I come and as I go, in the between time.
I try to layer peace behind, within, beneath, and all around my daily
tasks.
I try.
I try to keep the Idea of the Holy close at hand.
I try to be kind, considerate, helpful.
I practice anger management, anticipating and preparing,
so the beast cannot come through the anger door.
I sweeten myself with candy, books, and little daily pleasures,
like the New York Times and good coffee.
I strengthen myself with exercise and moral fortitude.
I dress nicely, just to please myself.

Mac Greene

I assert myself, just enough.
I apologize. I don't hold grudges.
I notice the good in people. I pay attention to sky, birds,
and little miracles.
Mindfulness. That's the new word.
But sometimes all of this and more is not enough.
Sometimes it's wasted effort, false sweetener, empty piety.

Some days, some weeks,
I'm a mean man for no good reason.
I have vague headaches. I clench my jaw.
My nerves jangle. The world abrades.
Nothing I do is right.
I embarrass myself.
I hurt the ones I love.
My shoulders tense. My gut strains.
My heart palpitates. My skin actually crawls.

Ominous.
It's a horror movie, something evil stirs in the suburbs.
The beast is looking over my shoulder, through my eyes.
It's blending into me.
I'm not myself.
Sarcasm curls my lips.
Road rage is the least of it.
I could kill.

Why?
Why is the beast claiming me?
What did I do?
Am I guilty?
Who will pay?

WHY NOT TALK ABOUT IT?

Holding onto the brittle, barely resolved pains
In places I need for walks, movement, waking up
My hips started their regular dialogue with me at 39.

I didn't get to have a baby. Timing, instability, bumpy
roads in marriage put me back onto family planning
despite my long held dream, envisioned as I cared for
the animals.

But 39 is when hormones spooned in to give big
swallows of disenchantment with becoming an aging
mom, adamant and intent upon repeating decade
old pursuits of maternity.

To my life's fortune, yoga mornings woke me gently
from My dreams, 8 a.m.'s, rainy Portland mornings to
open my View from the dashboard to the deep river
gorge, Hiking, best friend.

In the letting go, as unmarried and dogging toward 40,
I pronounced that I would be happier without children.

I saw the roads both stretched out in corpse pose.

Would I regret not having them? Would I more deeply
Resent having them. In my rest, after my practice,
Tears warmed my reclined cheeks with tangible answers.

Casey taught me the term for this 'wet practice.'
It's the cleaner spray on the windshield.
My hips ache less after another level of letting go.

I told my first husband, whom I remarried 5 years later,
I feel the loss down there, I ache in my hips
for that baby, I'm sore sometimes and now
I see what hurts.

We have a happy baby pose among us,
resting contentedly with vulnerable,
awkward limbs bellied up, and it's 5 years
Later, but I'm free for the next 45,
Lucky pair, still resolving.

POTTERY IS YOGA

The many gifts of inspiration
Flowing creativity through body & mind
Energy from these hands
fingertips knowing how hard to press
Opening possibilities
We are partners in the creative dance
Taking on new form
Ever evolving, courageous & joyful
Daring to go further, yet mindful
Seeing no boundaries
No cluttered thoughts
Bound together
The earth & me.

BREATHE DEEP

Deep Breath In
(awareness that I am here)

Deep Breath Out
(feeling that I have arrived)

Deep Breath In
(gratitude for my teachers)

Deep Breath Out
(wanting to give all of myself)

Deep Breath In
(an intense wave of desire)

Deep Breath Out
(letting it go)

Deep Breath In
(consumed by love)

Deep Breath Out
(becoming peace)

Deep Breath In
( )

Deep Breath Out
(MMMMMMMMM...)

VESSEL

You say teach me God's Song,
yet the music seems too simple,
the tone is the ocean,
the words are the thunder,
the song is the birds.

You say teach me of Giving,
yet it is done without doing,
my gold is joy,
my silver is wisdom,
my pearls are forgiveness.

You say teach me of Truth,
yet truth seems obscure,
caught between yes and no,
death and desire,
dusk and dawn.

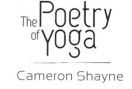

The Poetry of Yoga

Cameron Shayne

You say teach me of Art,
yet mine seems ordinary,
my colors comfort,
my strokes nourish,
my work endures.

You say teach me of Love,
yet mine seems indifferent,
my joy is your freedom,
my gaze is your reflection,
my kiss is true.

You say teach me to Worship,
yet mine seems foolish,
my prayer is my word,
my offering is myself,
my church is the earth.

You say teach me of Heaven,
yet mine seems too distant,
my king is the Son,
my God is in all,
my Kingdom is within.

TINY ASCETIC CAVE

Beside the River Ganga
I come upon a tiny cave,
with floor of sand,
woven mat for bed,
rounded stone for pillow,
light from the setting sun
glowing red within.
The river glints and gabbles
just beyond its mouth.
The falling light intensifies
the saffron tones of Rishikesh
as chant from a nearby ashram
resounds ecstatically.
Endless human ashes
from ghats upstream,
snuffed by the all-
embracing waters,
sweep by like silt
to occupy the mind.
A million miles in spirit
from the maddening roar
of the materialistic world!
I take a photo
to look at later:
tiny ascetic cave,
at the moment
unoccupied,
a long invisible finger
beckoning me
to come inside.

I WANT TO BE YOUR YOGA GIGOLO

I want to be your yoga gigolo,
your downward facing dog,
your sticky mat partner,
your cat and cow man.

I want to be your demonstration model,
your stick figure diagram,
your striking cobra, your kundalini serpent,
your warrior one, two, and three
your head and handstand man.

I want to be your cooing pigeon,
your uninhibited roaring lion,
your quivering unstrung arrow,
your deep-breathing man,

your crow, your crane,
your sleepy lily pad frog,
your ever-unfolding lotus,
the lord of your dance.

I want you to adjust me and adjust me again,
to set me straight in your entangling asana.
I want to open your chakras as you open mine.

I want to be the sun in your salutation,
the moon in your repose,
the flame in your meditation.
I want to be your yoga gigolo,
to see the fire in me in you
and the light in you in me.

The **Poetry** of **Yoga**

Richard James Allen

OUT OF SILENCE

(In memory of Swami Nirmalanda, the Silent Sage,
who practiced 'mauna,' or refraining from speaking)

If I were to speak
    If I were to
    open my mouth.

If I were to speak
    After all these years
    of inner quietude.

If I were to speak
    I would have
    no wish
    to speak
    just to or for myself.

            Words have
        a wider responsibility
        than I once realized.
            There isn't time
        to get caught in curlicues
        and tangles of abstraction
            and obscuration,
            in whirlpools
            of symbolism.

The Poetry
of Yoga

Richard James Allen

If I were to speak now
  It would be
  to give voice

  to the deeper resonance
  within us all.

        This is really
        the only voice

        we should be
        listening to,

        as it is the only one
        we can all share.

If I were to speak
  If you were to speak
  Let us speak.

The Poetry of Yoga

Erin Pillman

HEART SPACE

I am the Phoenix rising from the ashes
I am the sacred waters of rebirth
I am the fiery blaze of transformation
A vessel of inspired grace on Earth

I am the aching soul of every woman
I am the spiral rising to the sky
I am the beauty of your love's perfection
The who and what and where and when and why

I am the life, the death, and resurrection
I am the sacred whispers of your heart
I am the faithful joy that lives within you
The wisdom that the goddesses impart

I am a perfect mirror for your reflection
I am a dancing spirit in the trees
I am a magic spell for truth and healing
The ancient holy mother on her knees

I am the light that shimmers through the darkness
I am the mystic sitting on the hill
I am the symphony of imperfection
The part of you that's always calm and still

I am the fire burning in the temple
I am the child playing in the field
I am the noble heart of one who knows me
The art of knowing how to softly yield

The Poetry of Yoga

Erin Pillman

I am the feelings welling up inside you
I am the secrets floating on the breeze
I am the vital force that lives and breathes you
The universe, the lamppost, and the bees

I am the flowing waters of the river
I am the music singing in your veins
I am the dream that you are always dreaming
The always ever after that remains

I am the angel walking here beside you
I am the kindness smiling through the pain
I am the eyes that love and understand you
The rolling hills of Italy and Spain

I am the favorite son and favorite daughter
I am the simple truth you'll always know
I am the cause for every celebration
The fruits you reap for every word you sow

I am the shining sun beyond the rainstorm
I am the clouds, the heavens, and the Earth
I am the solemn prayers of those who feel me
The journey home you've been on since your birth

I am the lotus flower and the demon
I am the all and everything between
I am the loving mother who beholds you
The king, the prince, the princess, and the queen

The Poetry of Yoga

Erin Pillman

I am the brilliant sparkle in the snowflake
I am the silver lining in the cloud
I am the stunning colors of the sunset
The courage and the strength to live out loud

I am the unexpected and the subtle
I am the promise and the guarantee
I am the activation of your power
The simple truth of your divinity

I am the silly smile of an infant
I am the path of true awakening
I am the pure devotion of a servant
The glimmer and the glow of mystery

I am the dainty footprints of the fairy
I am the earthly roots that nourish
I am the whirling stardust in your eyes
And you are Me, and I am always You.

FLOATING ON THAT

Six pm yoga class Tuesday one week
To the day since we buried my father
Ninety minutes holding breathing
Sweating intense then Savasana - release
Let it go there is so much magnificence
Near the ocean waves are coming in
Waves coming in Pachelbel alleluias
Tender as tears that still have not come.

So much magnificence and Dad at the beach
Lost his hat in the waves coming in and
My little girl heart feared we couldn't
Buy another for his bald head Daddy
Picked me Christmas Day crying
Three-year-old tears fell asleep in his
Strong young man arms khaki pants
Father instinct knew what to do then
He drifted away like that hat carried off with the
Waves coming in out of reach so magnificent.

Now on my mat the lights dim I am floating
On that sea the warm rises and swells
He is floating there with me peaceful arms
Outstretched fingers reaching for mine
Alleluias like an altar call coming giant sob
Pushes up from the ocean floor softens
Like the crest of a wave as it curls wants
To break but it flattens and moves on still
I float he is there I am held we are all of us held so
Magnificent floating together on that same great sea.

SAME GREAT SEA

PRATYAHARA

Draw tight the shroud
Become enveloped

Thirst released
unquenchable

Speech abandoned
inadequate

Pleasures left behind
redundant

Passage into Everything
Requires this Nothing

The delicious beauty
of an empty bowl

THE EIGHT GREAT LIMBS

Make this prayer:
ashta-anga
go deep inside
from my heart
to my soul
through my skin

gut the place
crack it open
expose the rot
scrape it away

Do not fear these words
Trust completely
Rumi was right
Demolition always turns out to be renovation

This rebuild will exceed all the visions of men
Even with just a foundation poured
And some basic framing in place
The glory of your new arena will show itself

Now imagine dancing in the finished structure....

The Poetry of Yoga

Andréa Vincent

UNION

Breath and body move as one
Salutation to the moon and sun
in the natural flow from night to day
dark and light unite and interplay
with every fiber of my being
I feel an inner sense of freeing
as the energy begins to surge
the elements meet and merge
Earth, ether, water, air, fire
on cresting waves dance ever higher
each stretching breath lifts to inspire
as grace fills my cup to overflowing
ineffable joy knows innately where it's going
following an inner urge
melting in nothingness to emerge
in the endless eternal heart's embrace
of spirit beyond time and space
Ever flowing ever still
its fathomless peace
will never cease
to thrill
as I fill
with the bliss
of a kiss
to my very core
from the One I endlessly adore
you are who you were waiting for
sweet blessed union with Forevermore

FAITH

Totally

from which

my breath

originates

does my

trust

remain

The Poetry
of Yoga

Eve Eliot

MEDITATION FOR TEDIOUS HOUSEHOLD TASKS

Emptying the dishwasher
Or vacuuming the carpet
Washing dishes or
Sweeping the floor.

Every time you place a dish back in its place,
every spoon nestling, think of one other person.
Dedicate each swipe of the broom or sponge to another person.

Perhaps that person is engaged in the same kind of task,
feeling impatient.

Perhaps that person is homeless in Haiti.
Perhaps that person doesn't have a single spoon,
or floor.

This way you won't have to feel agitated,

The Poetry
of Yoga

Eve Eliot

rushing to get these tedious tasks accomplished
so you can go on to greater things,
to spiritual fulfillment,
to philanthropic goals,
to connection,
belonging.

You can make all that happen
as you place the knives back in their drawer.
You can connect with your Aunt Mabel
who is in the hospital five states away,
just by thinking of her while you stack the clean dish-
es in the cabinet,
one by one, quietly, gently.

Your heart can fill.
You can be at peace.
Your house, organized.
Your mind, soothed.

The Poetry of Yoga

Mikelle Terson

IF EVERYTIME I
WORRIED

If every time I worried,
I read the biography of a great person instead
I just know, I'd be Washing tons of garbage from my head
I'd soothe the monkey on my shoulder
Leave niggling fears behind
Fill my skull with inspiration
Be more conscious of my mind

Cause I've been Lincoln lately
I too have a dream, Martin
To be Queen, of my cranial domain to saturate my nerves
With thoughts of those more brilliant and more sane

Yeah, if every time I worried, I read the biography of a great
person instead,
I'd get so relaxed
I'd kick back,
Cross my legs and Sai Baba sip a lemon Schweitzer
Have a few crackers spread with cured Madame
sprinkled with a little Jonas Salk
follow it up with some chocolate Rilke

Franklin, I've Ben
pondering
the key could be for me
to spend my time
with some Einstein (relatively speaking),

reduce my early trauma
with the words of Dalai Lama

let Shakespeare sonnet through me
and fall in Love with Rumi
Read the writings of Tagore
See beauty Helen Keller saw
get God-drunk with Hafiz,
comprehend what Hawkins says

If every time I worried, I read the biography of
a great person instead
I think, my troubles would all be Ghan di
Jesus, I'd be feeling so much Buddha

And maybe I'd be nicer to the Mother... uh... Teresa
That cut me off in traffic.

GURUS

Gurus -
my pink, ripe naked feet
blithely dawn
after many kalpas
of dark, stifled longings

These gurus know something I don't.

The Tarahumara Indians glide through
the canyons of the Sierra Madres
just like the ancestors did -
shoeless - more or less

And the yogis reverently rub their paws with oil.
They stand in the wisdom of mountain pose,
the original ground of being,
awakening abeyant discrimination

The barefoot sisters walked from Maine to Georgia
and back again - barefoot

Barefoot!

The Poetry of Yoga

Loretta Pyles

No shoes
or socks
or flip flops
or boots

An imprint of my indigo hooves
remains
on birth papers
or maybe a golden-framed certificate

Tiny, baby feet

Slowly became prisoners of shoes
And fear
And swallowed silences

Feet!
Gurus of ten thousand paths,
And endless sources of being and doing,
Show me the light!
I bow down to you.

Om namo.

MY ROAMING OM

today my om roamed
around this hot town!

we went out of body
and to yoga
floated through the park
and saw the sights
from the third eye
top o' the intuition!

today, my om roamed
across the country
oceans, atoms
and into far away places
igniting light and sound,
into the dark and quiet,
but we need them too,
my om balanced that quotient...

we also penetrated hearts
in the immediate vicinity, locally
this om and me became contagious,
electrical magic
infecting people
with their very own universal vibration,
your very own
personal primordial sound vibration, my friend...

Ava Bird

om and i got to walkin'
around this great town,
holy mother earth,
we entered the consciousness
of our listeners,
we wanted to share

but had no expectations
of returning Om's,
only committing ourselves
activating our own hearts
electric cell magic
and hope others jump on the bandwagon
to sing and moan 'Om'
we rode the spiritual super highway,

this Om and I
floating on freeways,
expressways,
our community sponsored Om,
Om parks
Om soup kitchens,
pure organic and raw sounds
roots and seeds,

simply, our souls home,
roaming in our euphoric moan,
the freeway home,
Om!

The Poetry of Yoga

Teniesha Kessler

CORPSE POSE

I watched a fly die
while in downward dog,
its posture perfectly reclined
and flailing legs stretched straight
reaching for reincarnation
like sun salutations cycling
again and again and again
until the practice slows,
breath steadies,
heartbeat dips into serenity,
and eyes close
for corpse pose,
bridging consciousness and sleep
as muscles twitch slightly
just like the fly,
whose final buzz echoed
Namasté.

HOME PRACTICE

I do standing poses
I am in a room filled with drums
Everything hurts. I hug in
I root down, I root up, organic energy
I engage my muscles in side angle
I make sure my muscles don't move off the bones,
I am softening, I fill up with air
side body long, open to grace
Inner, outer spiral, tuck the tail bone, Mula-bandha
This is not a linear thing
Triangle pose
I am not in my house
I hug my feet towards each other
my hamstring is safe
Sometimes I think my front leg needs more outer spiral
I vacillate between the two
One is right and both are right
Down dog
I get my arms in the right place
head of the arm bones moving forward
The muscles attaching the scapula feel funny
I back off
Sometimes I think I can engage my muscles right off the bone
not a good thing, I soften again, breathe in to the back body
I draw up from the knee caps
thighs pushing back, upwards behind me,
protecting the psoas during the lunge pose
Reverse warrior
I go from side angle prep to reverse warrior
Back and forth like Elena says
I twist in a lunge, my arm to the sky
I keep it simple
That was yesterday
Today I will sit in meditation
inner spiral my thigh, outer spiral my shin
So my good knee wont hurt

START WITH
ANY KIND OF PAUSE

Start with any kind of pause. To stop moving forward, to re-
lax the clenched circle of possession that has hardened the
edges of how you meet what is wanted. To feel needs hover
like mist, and lift. The bones sink into the chair. Eyes relax
back into the skull. Sounds become spatial again, and breath
breathes you.

During any activity will do. Maybe it is easier when alone,
in the midst of self-care. When the hand holding the
washcloth feels it is washing itself. When the hands
preparing food relax into the pleasure of hands being food.
To fall asleep with one hand behind the head, and the other
over the sternum. To melt your holding away, held by hands
having no complex intention.

It's easier when alone: this is what the ascetics
discovered. Let the mirror neurons relax their engagement
with the angst of others, and reflect the peace of things, of
flesh. The peace of things reveals you as a piece of all things.
This all happens before and beyond language. The sentence
of the mind can suddenly need no completion.

Suddenly, thought does not need to carry out its
sentence. The page of the world is sufficient.

Josh Schrei

THE GIFT OF LONGING

Oh heart of all the world

Of all the many verses
in the long and wayward song of
my search for union

I remember first
the one in which I
sang of separation

and with my words
cut a line between the edges of my self
and your sweet sky

Heart of all the world,
sweet source of all forgiving
it was at the very moment
that I called you "mine"

that you became small
a mere organ of task and function
And I became small with you

cast forth like a lost child who carries with him
the clothes on his back
and a crumpled paper map with rough directions home

Yet it was in that same moment
of the singing of the verse of separation
that you gave me the gift of longing
and now the songs that I sing are songs of union
and the spaces that I walk are the wide and open halls
of the house of the heart of all the world

The Poetry of Yoga

Josh Schrei

Heart of all sweetness,
great honeycomb of stars

I am a blind singer
with a broken lute
Who carries only the gift of longing

And if I had not been divided
would I ever have been able to know your love?

Seven billion hearts
Lord,
sing the song of longing
if we had not been divided
would we have known your love?

Between this moment
and the time of great rejoicing
is the space where all songs are born

That is the space
of the arising of ten thousand stars

the place where together we
find the one space
that is called Heart

that is called Love.

FEATHER

My burden was a stone
That you showed me was a hammer
That you taught me to swing
So I could forge the great chain
That leads straight to your heart
The heart of your sweetness
The everlasting light
My Lord, Oh great Lord

My burden was a wasteland
That you showed me was a garden
That you taught me to care for
To grow this great bounty
That comes straight from your heart
The heart of your sweetness
The everlasting light
My Lord, Oh great Lord

My burden was a hole
That you showed me was a well
That you taught me to draw from
To fill the great vessel
With the waters of your heart
The heart of your sweetness
The everlasting light
My Lord, Oh Great Lord

As a man takes a hammer
And he pounds this raw metal,
As a man takes a spade

Josh Schrei

And he digs and he sows,
As a man takes a vessel
And he fills it with water,
Oh he fills it with the water
Of the everlasting source;

Then that man be a servant
Who holds gold beyond measure
That man be held fast
By the light of the World
That man picks his fruit
From the only true garden
That man fills his cup
At the everlasting source

My burden was a fire
That you showed me was a lantern
That you taught me to ignite
To cast light on the road
That leads straight to your heart

Now that it is lit,
May it stay so forever
May it be as a lighthouse
For all ships that founder
May it lead them to the harbor
At the heart of your sweetness
Oh the great harbor
Your everlasting light

My Lord, Oh Great Lord

ON OCCUPYING THE PRESENT

can you receive these words
through your intellectual faculties without
being constrained by thoughts or getting caught
in the web of analysis?
are you willing to examine this together with me by feeling your
way through these letters and forgiving these words
for conjuring up relics of your own experience,
which is inherently limited?
words also feel like exhausted and unappreciated
workers at times.
i thank you for offering your eyes and your imagination.

share space

dissolve barriers of yours and mine so we can walk together
not in an ordered line but to sever notions
that property is personal

space is personal in that i fill it with presence of mine
and time is of the essence when i occupy it with
presence of mind
dialogue yields re-purposing of how we conceive
of possessions when we understand that they are temporal
today there are displaced obsessions on concrete,
tangible things
i'm thirsty for the feeling i get when awareness
is consecrated to the spaces between

The Poetry of Yoga

Jamie Rothard

it feels like utopia can be accessible without so much
trying to make it
and creation so much more fluid when the ego
steps out of the way
appreciate all the energy that would be released
once the anxiety of what's yours and mine has ceased
to seize such a tight grip on our notion of worth
our interconnection is a more enduring infrastructure
than metal bars forced into the earth
to support misguided projections
i want to free up the energy reserved for protection
and self-preservation and distill it down to what is ours,
communicated through meditation

i've envisioned masses of silent 'mobs' walking together
holding candles and looking out at the world with soft eyes
and somewhere in there is the wordless answer
to what my core cries out for to achieve
communication without tirelessly speaking,
understanding without over-thinking
and acceptance that perfection is together
in the present state
yet some will do or take anything for a glimpse
of what that potential could feel like
we barter with chemicals to alter consciousness
and i understand the intent to dissolve the daily buildup
of playing along with a game we didn't invent
but still perpetuate

The Poetry of Yoga

Jamie Rothard

and responsibility is an essential element,
too often substituted for with self-hate
our interconnectedness is an inevitable reality
while we've magnified the role of duality
so that we can't even appreciate its merits
letting opposites be pinned against each other,
we resist completion like we're scared of it

and we'd stop fearing each other when we cease
to fear what's at our core
competition is obsolete; the futility of keeping score
in a game we play against ourselves
simultaneously, living is a divine comedic paradox
because there is so much that living in the tangible teaches me
when i'm not hell-bent on controlling it with my mind
my physical body yields a beautiful form
when i don't force it to take the shape of a temporal idea of mine

what's there to lose in believing the same goes with nature?

everything, if i'm attached to force
nothing, if i believe in the perfected order
nature has to run her course.

yet i cannot find peace in any ideology, substance or system
of belief that i can yield to.
the paradox is i've already reached the destination, and it is Love.

The Poetry
of Yoga

Tracy Dominick
James

ONE BREATH

With one breath
I hold myself in this moment.
On the finest edge
of a deep inhale borne of
sturdy blood and bone,
I set my bow.

I wait for the debris and dust
to settle.
I wait for the drumbeat
to slow.
I wait for the tangled howl of the insatiable world
to give way to a gossamer whisper.
I wait for the chaos
to order.
On the edge of this pulsating breath,
the rhythm of my matrix sets my course
for one point ahead,
and I wait.

Fear, be gone from me.
Doubt, lay down your sword.
Your tongues are coarse,
your murmurings deceptive.
I spring from a more vital language;
I understand now who I am.

I am neither the debris nor the dust.
I am neither the drum nor the howl.
I am neither the chaos nor the order.

I am the branch that will bend without breaking.
I am the sigh of the stretching string.
I am but the moment and the breath;
they are all, and everything.

And on the edge of that moment,
I draw back the bowstring,
reach bravely forward towards life and

let that one breath
go.

EAST VILLAGE
ENLIGHTENMENT

She
gets up to go to the bathroom
leaving me on an East Village fire escape
with colored lights and tree fronds tickling my cheeks
as they suck down seltzer.
She's gone,
and I stare at the fronds, waving in the early summer breeze
and my third eye opens like a golden red light
I'm strung with the bulbs,
waltzing wide in the wind.
My atoms sparkle with night air.

I wondered if someone had spiked my water,
felt a moment of panic flush my face,
What Is Wrong With Me?

Nothing.
That's the point.
She and I chewed our problems so much
they crumbled like butter cookie and
I Know,
for this moment
the miracle of my life,
which if I could just remember,
would not be beating up this way.

I wonder
is anyone on retreat
sending me metta in large bundles?

The Poetry of Yoga

Sarah Herrington

Which ex-boyfriend is thinking of me
in one of their Brooklyn apartments
sending me the love they forgot?

But, no, this wasn't about them.
This was just a random moment of release,
of expansion, of oneness—

maybe the result of hours of moving meditation
on the yoga mat,
or hours of lucid dreaming,
or hours of soul searching in the eyes and sights of the City,
or hours of writing questions in the form of poems.

"What are you doing?"
she asks,
my head in the bushes.

"Thinking."
She sits,
and we serve each other more problems on cold dishes,
the human ritual of anti-grace
I chew on the tough bits,
she licks up the crumbs.

But underneath I feel a deep sweet humming
in my heart like chocolate on the tongue.
That part is bored of this conversation
and wants to toast it instead
that part is real love.

SHOES

In church, fancy shoes were worn
scuff-free shoes, bejeweled shoes, high-heeled shoes
teetering toward heaven.
I felt bare wood between my fingers
holding the back of the pew in front of me
as I slipped off one shoe at a time,
shrinking in height next to my Grandmother,
who was apparently trying to reach God with large hats.
Now.
At the mosque down the street from my apartment,
men take off their work boots
in favor of socks or thin sandals
to bow down toward the East River.
Men,
sometimes spilling out of the mosque
and onto the street itself,
barefoot,
fabric knees kissing pavement again and again.

The Poetry of Yoga

Sarah Herrington

In the meditation hall,
my socks scuff in walking meditation,
rolling through bones and pressure points,
stilling the mind
God, where do you want me to go?
And how should I get there?
In motorcycle boots, red-high stilettos, bare toes?
I follow white Kenneth Cole cottoned heels
moving slowly in front of me.
Toe, heel, heel, toe.

On the spongy yoga mat,
my barest of feet grip and release,
leaving small prayer prints as unique
as our own inner language.
My toes polished, or not.
Sometimes they go upside down, standing on air.

God must have ears bigger than my downstairs neighbor,
to hear all the heel clicking and toe padding and sock scuffing.
All those barefoot intentions and well-heeled thoughts.

The Poetry of Yoga

Sarah Herrington

IMAGINE YOUR BREATH HAS FINGERS

in savasana

let your wings fall through the earth

dangling off your shoulder-blades

like broken compass arrows

growing in all directions

as much as you let go

you are supported

acceptance is not complacency

but clear seeing

a motor of change

Focus on the exhale

the inhale will take care of itself

you have choices / Choose.

SAVASANA

I step softly into the serene savannah
Its familiar silence envelopes me and I am still.

Moments before
A stampede of thundering thoughts approached,
A cloud of dust billowing in their wake.

This happens every time.

I close my eyes and wait for it to pass,
Hoping this time I will not get trapped
Amongst the aggressive, tightly formed herd
And carried away.

Jolted from the infinite openness of eternity
Back into the loud, unyielding minutiae of the day.

The thunderous thicket of lists,
Demands, obligations, guilt, remorse
Shoulds and Shouldn'ts
Hurtle past, and this time,
I resist their magnetic pull.
I wait calmly, abide, and once the dust settles,
The quiet bliss of the savannah returns.

ACKNOWLEDGEMENTS

My deepest gratitude to our ancestors, upon your shoulders we stand, and may you continue to use me as a vessel for your spirit and passion, strength and wisdom, beauty and grace. This book is your reflection and now our shared dreams.

This project is bigger than just one person, and honestly, it's bigger than just a book. There have been so many people involved in helping bring it to fruition. *The Poetry of Yoga* started as a workshop series until my dearest Katie Capano planted the seed in my brain to turn it into a book. Over the few years, from idea to manifestation, she has always been my first opinion. From there it was a snowball of amazing volunteers, supporters and kindred spirits helping to make it a reality.

Indispensable through this whole process is Laura Berol. In the beginning of 2011, she came on as a One Common Unity fellow, assigned to this fundraising initiative. She has helped manage and direct communications for the project, including countless correspondence, organizing of databases and outreach trackers. She was the only one, other than me, who read all the submissions that came in through our website. Most importantly, she has been unbelievably gracious with her time and heart.

Also, great thanks to Bethany Wichman and Chivonnie Gius-Meekins, for continued support in the office and believing in my dream that this book will raise money for One Common Unity youth programs! Interns Ariel Saidman and Albatoul Basha were instrumental during the infant stages of this project.

In the final phase, Sascha Rossaint, was tremendous and meticulous in completing the layout and design for Volume 2. His creativity and vision shined a whole new light on the project. Bill Tipper pushed in the clutch, yet again, when he offered another one of his gorgeous photographs for the front cover. His work is divine (www.billtipper.com). A special thank you

The Poetry of Yoga

to Sarah of Massey Media who spent a year helping me sculpt a story arc and National Tour for the workshop series back in 2010. Jill Kianka of Vico Rock Media provided amazing web development and design of *The Poetry of Yoga* site.

The wonderful Erin Weston worked diligently to record and produce audio and video. And her colleague Michael Lindley assisted her in putting together the informational video announcing the book launch.

As I burned the midnight oil, there were numerous people who stepped up by helping with suggestions, edits, revisions, recording audio, producing media broadcasts, and PR including: Utamu Onaje, Sia Tiambi Barnes, Doug Swenson, Radhakrishna Kasat, Chelsea Edgett, Mikuak Rai, Sharon Gannon, Sianna Sherman, Ellie Walton, Jessica Durivage, Diane Ferraro, Rod Stryker, Joanne Jagoda, Bob Weisenberg, Shiva Rea, Debra & Ian Mishalove, Lalita Noronha-Blob, Patricia Busbee, Luke Shors and Madhuri Kasat.

Infinite love to my parents and family who have always been supportive of all my crazy ideas; and, of course, to all of you! The hundreds upon hundreds of people who sent in poetry, shared the word with friends, and lent voice to this massive project.

ABOUT THE EDITOR

HawaH teaches about solutions to violence and ways to peace, and has traveled to over 30 countries to facilitate interactive workshops, dialogues, perform poetry, teach yoga, and speak with those interested in creating a caring, sustainable, and equitable world.

He has worked as an *AmeriCorps* big brother in one of Washington, D.C.'s most under-resourced neighborhoods, and also as an R.F.K. Memorial Foundation fellow as a special representative to the United Nations and the *World Conference Against Racism*.

HawaH is co-founder of *One Common Unity*, a non-profit organization that inspires non-violent culture through education, arts, and media. For 3 years he directed the Peaceable Schools Program in D.C.'s largest public high school, specifically developing leadership skills of youth and assisting them in dealing with trauma through Alternatives to Violence, Deep Breathing & Yoga classes. He holds certifications in both *Sivananda* and *Jivamukti* Yoga schools.

Over the years, HawaH has trained thousands of teachers in the principles of social-emotional learning and is a regularly featured speaker, performer and workshop presenter for *People to People International, the Congressional Youth Leadership Council* and the *Children's Defense Fund's Freedom Schools*.

A spoken word poet known as *Everlutionary*, and an artist of a diverse collection of paintings and photographs, he has authored four books, produced three documentary films, and released two CD's.

The Poetry of Yoga

OTHER WORKS
BY HAWAH

BOOKS
Trails: Trust Before Suspicion (non-fiction travel novel)   (2001)
Escape Extinction (essays and poetry)   (2003)
zerONEss (poetry and prose)   (2005)

DOCUMENTARY FILMS
A Weigh With Words   (2007)
The MLK Streets Project   (2011)
Fly By Light: Discover Your True Nature   (2013)

CDS
Survival for All Of Us   (2008)
CALL   (2010)

ONLINE
www.EVERLUTIONARY.net   (2000)

Fifty percent of proceeds from this book are donated
to One Common Unity, a grassroots 501(c)3 non-profit
organization. Since the year 2000, they have been supporting
and inspiring a movement for peace education and the building
of a nonviolent culture through music, media and art.

For more information about their pioneering work please visit:

www.OneCommonUnity.org

the poetry of YOGA

www.ThePoetryOfYoga.com
www.Facebook.com/ThePoetryOfYoga

poetryofyoga@gmail.com